The Teenager's Guide to Bridge

ALSO BY ROBERT B. EWEN

Opening Leads
Doubles for Takeout, Penalties and Profit in Contract Bridge
Preemptive Bidding
Contract Bridge: A Concise Guide
Getting It Together: A Guide to Modern
Psychological Analysis
Introductory Statistics for the Behavioral Sciences (*co-author*)
Introductory Statistics Workbook

The Teenager's Guide to Bridge

ROBERT B. EWEN

DODD, MEAD & COMPANY · NEW YORK

Library of Congress Cataloging in Publication Data

Ewen, Robert B   date
    The teenager's guide to bridge.

    SUMMARY: An introduction to the terminology,
rules, strategy, and techniques of contract bridge.
    1. Contract bridge—Juvenile literature.
[1. Bridge (Game)] I. Title.
GV1282.3.E924   795.4'15   74-11435
ISBN 0-396-07147-3

Contents

The Teenager's Guide
to Bridge

Let's Play Bridge!

Welcome to the fascinating world of contract bridge! This great game offers you:

A unique test of your skill, memory, and ability to plan ahead.

A chance to draw shrewd deductions from various kinds of clues.

An element of luck similar to the excitement of "hitting the jackpot."

An intriguing challenge in effective teamwork.

So many new situations that you won't get tired of it, even if you play it for the rest of your life.

In addition, bridge requires a minimum of equipment, and it does *not* have to be played for money to be enjoyable—no small advantages in this era of runaway inflation! For these reasons, bridge has millions of devoted enthusiasts all over the world.

This book is your invitation to join them.

STARTING A BRIDGE GAME

THE PLAYERS

Bridge requires four players, each of whom sits at one side of a square table. For ease of reference, it is customary to use compass directions to identify the players:

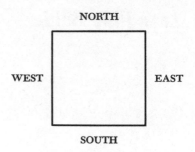

North and South are **partners**, as are East and West. Partnerships can be determined by agreement; or, if everyone wants to partner the best player (or the prettiest girl), each player randomly draws a card from the deck and the two players with the highest cards team up against the two players with the lowest cards (a procedure called "cutting for partners").

In bridge, all actions proceed *clockwise* around the table. If West happens to be the first to do something (such as deal, bid, or play a card), then North is next to do the same, and he is followed in turn by East and then South.

THE DECK

Bridge uses the standard 52-card deck, which has four suits: Spades (♠), Hearts (♡), Diamonds (◇), and

Clubs (♣). Each suit contains 13 cards: Ace (A), the highest-ranking; King (K); Queen (Q); Jack (J); 10; 9; 8; 7; 6; 5; 4; 3; and 2 (deuce), the lowest-ranking. The five highest-ranking cards in each suit (A, K, Q, J, and 10) are called **honors**, while the remaining lower cards (9 through 2) are called **spot cards**.

THE DEAL

The action is started by the player drawing the highest card during the cut for partners (or, if partnerships were determined by agreement, during a special cut held at this point). He takes the entire deck and shuffles (mixes) it thoroughly, making sure that no one can see any of the cards, and then allows the player on his right to "cut" the deck (take about the top half of the deck and place it on the table, and then put what was formerly the bottom of the deck on top of the pile). He then gives (**deals**) the top card, face down, to the player at his *left*; deals the second card to his partner; and continues clockwise around the table, one card at a time, until the entire deck has been distributed and each player has 13 cards (his **hand**).*

Out of courtesy to the dealer, no one should pick up any cards until the deal is completed. And when you do pick up your cards, be sure to hold them so that no one else can see them! All your skill and effort will be wasted if you let the opponents catch a glimpse of your hand and thereby make a sensational (and profitable!) play.

* Many bridge players like to speed things up by having the dealer's partner shuffle a second deck while the deal is going on. Thus, when South is dealing, North shuffles a second deck and then places it to his right or near West, who will be the next dealer.

Each deal consists of two parts: The **bidding** (also called the **auction**) takes place first, and is followed by the **play**. When the play has been completed, everyone is out of cards—and hence ready for the next deal.

OVERVIEW OF A DEAL OF BRIDGE

THE BIDDING (AUCTION)

During the bidding, the four suits have a rank order that is of particular importance, and there is also a denomination called **Notrump** that outranks any suit:

DENOMINATION	RANK
Notrump (NT)	Highest
Spades (♠)	Second highest
Hearts (♡)	Third highest
Diamonds (◊)	Fourth highest
Clubs (♣)	Lowest

The two highest-ranking suits, Spades and Hearts, are called the **major** suits; while the lowly Diamond and Club suits are referred to as the **minor** suits.

To keep bridge books from running to huge numbers of pages (and dollars), bridge writers report a player's cards in the following concise way:

SOUTH
♠ A
♡ K Q 6 3
◊ 7 5 4 2
♣ J 10 9 8

This is considerably easier than saying that "South has the Ace of Spades; the King, Queen, Six, and Three of Hearts; the Seven, Five, Four, and Two of Diamonds; and the Jack, Ten, Nine, and Eight of Clubs." As an aid to memory, the suits are always presented in rank order, and the rank of the cards within each suit decreases as you read from left to right. When you actually pick up and sort your cards, however, it's highly desirable to alternate colors instead of sticking to suit rank order:

Confusing a Heart with a Diamond or a Spade with a Club can have fatal consequences, and this arrangement will help to prevent such catastrophes.

After sorting his cards, the dealer begins the auction. If he feels that his hand is strong enough, he makes an appropriate **bid**; if not, he says "**pass.**" The player on his left then either bids or passes, and the auction proceeds clockwise around the table and continues until there are *three consecutive passes*. Every player, however, is entitled to at least one chance to bid; so if (say) you are East, and South deals and passes and West and North also pass, you *are* allowed to bid if you wish. (This is the only exception to the rule that three consecutive passes end the auction.) If you also elect to pass, the deal is thrown in (**passed out**) and a new deal is begun.

The "three consecutive pass" rule provides an important element of strategy, for it *prevents any player from being assured of a second chance to bid.* Thus, if South is your partner and makes a bid of some kind, the auction may well end before he gets another chance—as will happen if West, you (North), and East all pass. Since it is usually *not* possible to accomplish all of one's objectives in a single bid, a player often depends on his partner to keep the auction from ending too soon. Therefore, one of the fascinating aspects of bridge is that you can't base your decision to bid or pass solely on the cards that you hold. You must also know when your partner expects you to keep the ball rolling by making a bid (a **forcing** situation), and when you can safely pass—and risk letting the auction come to an end—without driving your partner to hara-kiri (a **non-forcing** situation).

To avoid egregious blunders, you should pay close attention to everyone's calls while the auction is under way. If you do happen to need a reminder, however, you are allowed to ask for a **review of the bidding** whenever it is *your turn to bid.* When you make this request, one of your opponents must repeat all previous calls (including passes) in the order in which they were made.

THE PLAY

Starting the play. When the bidding has ended (and provided that the deal has not been passed out), the play begins. The bidding designates one player as the **de-**

clarer, and the person to his *left* starts things off by selecting any card in his hand and placing it face up in the center of the table. (This very first play is called the **opening lead**.) After the opening lead has been made, the declarer's partner places his *entire hand face up on the table*, with each suit in a separate column:

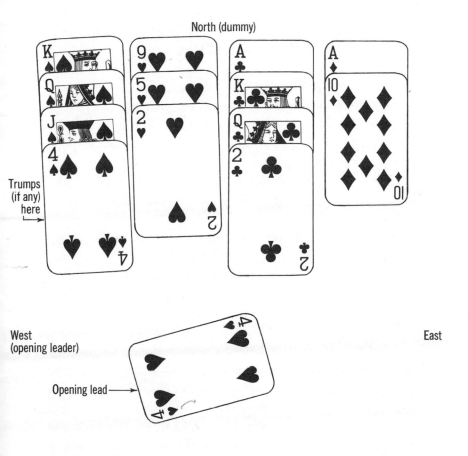

North (dummy)

Trumps
(if any)
here

West
(opening leader)

East

Opening lead ——▸

South (declarer)

If the bidding has designated one suit as the **trump suit**, it is placed at *declarer's left*. Colors are alternated to prevent confusion and eyestrain, and the rank of cards within each suit decreases as declarer reads from top to bottom.

The declarer's partner (North, in our example) will have nothing at all to do for the rest of this deal, and his hand is appropriately called the **dummy**. The declarer (here, South) will have the fun and challenge of handling the play for both partners.

Tricks. When the dummy has been revealed, the declarer selects and removes one card from it and places this card near the opening lead that is sitting in the center of the table. The next player in clockwise order (East, in our example) now places one of his cards face up in the middle of the table; and, lastly, the remaining player (the declarer) plays a card. The group of four cards accumulated in this fashion is called a **trick**.

Any player is allowed to see all of the cards that have been played to the trick in progress. In fact, anyone may examine the *immediately preceding* trick *until a member of his partnership has played to the next trick*, after which it is too late and memory must suffice.

Leads. Each trick is won by one player, and he then **leads** (plays first) to the next trick. For example, let's suppose that South has captured the first trick. He picks up the four cards, groups them into a single neat packet, and places them face down off on one side where they will not be in the way. South then leads to the next trick by selecting any card in his hand and placing it face up in the center of the table, and play proceeds clockwise until each player has contributed a card in turn. (That is, West plays next, declarer then selects a card from dummy, and East plays last.) This trick is then gathered in by a member of the winning side, and the player who won the trick leads to the next trick. Play continues in this fashion until all the cards are gone; and since everyone has 13 cards and contributes one of them to each trick, there will always be a total of 13 tricks in each deal.

On any one deal, only one member of a partnership should gather up and keep the tricks that they have won, so that the total will be easy to spot at any given moment. Dummy, as always, is out of it, and declarer always collects the tricks for his side.

Note that declarer *must* lead from his own hand when it won the previous trick, and *must* lead from dummy when it won the previous trick; seeing both hands does *not* give him freedom of choice. This implies that it can be a matter of some skill for declarer to win a given trick in the hand that will produce the most benefit by leading to the next trick.

Following suit. The leader to a trick is free to play any card in his hand. The other players, however, must "follow the leader" for the duration of that trick by *playing a card of the same suit as the one led*; that is, they must **follow suit** if they can. Thus, if North leads to a trick and chooses to play a Heart, East, South, and West must each play a Heart if they have one. If (say) East has several Hearts, he is free to play whichever one he wishes; while if he has no Hearts at all (either because he was never dealt any, or because he played all his Hearts on previous tricks), he may then play *any* card in his hand.

How tricks are won. A trick is won by the *highest card of the suit led* that is played to that particular trick. Sometimes the bidding will designate one suit as the **trump suit**, in which case *any card of the trump suit outranks any card of any other suit.* This means that on those occasions when you are able to play a trump, you will win the trick unless someone else plays a *higher trump.* If a card is played that is *not* of the suit led and *not* a trump, that card—called a **discard**—*cannot possibly win the trick.*

Let's look at some examples, ignoring for the moment the question of which unfortunate soul happens to be the dummy:

Example 1: Spades are trumps

WEST:
Leads ♡ 7.

Let's assume that West won the previous trick, and therefore leads to this one. He may choose any card in his hand, and (no doubt for some clever reason) selects the Seven of Hearts.

NORTH:
Plays ♡ 3.

North is next, and must play a Heart if he has one. He plays a very small Heart; so he either cannot, or doesn't want to, fight for this trick.

EAST:

Plays ♡ J.

East plays next, and must also follow suit if he can. Either he doesn't think that his partner's medium-sized Heart will win the trick, or he very much wants to lead to the next trick, or the Jack is his only Heart. However . . .

SOUTH:

Plays ♡ Q.

South plays last to this trick, and he too is required to follow suit. Paying close attention to the previous plays, he shrewdly decides to play the Queen of Hearts.

Result: South wins the trick, because his card was the highest one of the suit led. The fact that the Ace and King of Hearts are even higher doesn't matter, since they were not played to this trick; and the fact that Spades are trumps also turns out to be irrelevant, since everyone had to follow suit (and therefore could not play a trump).

South actually held the Ace of Hearts when this trick took place, and his play of the Queen was very well-reasoned. Since he was last to play to the trick, he could see that the Queen would suffice to win it. Therefore, there was no reason to expend the powerful Ace; so he saved it, and won another trick with it later on. And since each deal consist of 13 tricks but only four Aces, it is usually essential to win tricks with smaller cards in order to succeed at the bridge table!

Example 2: Notrump (there is no trump suit)

EAST:
Leads ◊ 5.

In this example, East has won the previous trick. He can play any card in his hand, and he chooses the Five of Diamonds.

SOUTH:
Plays ♡ 6.

This play shows that South has no Diamonds at all, since otherwise he would have to follow suit. He is therefore allowed to play any of his cards, and he selects the Six of Hearts. (A play like South's, where he neither follows suit nor plays a trump, is called a **discard**.)

WEST:
Plays ♠ 9.

West discards the Nine of Spades, so he also must be out of Diamonds.

NORTH:
Plays ♣ A.

North also has no Diamonds, and he discards the Ace of Clubs—a painful waste presumably caused by dire necessity!

Result: East wins the trick, because he played the highest card *of the suit led.* Even North's Ace can't save the day for his side, since it isn't in the same suit led by East. Thus, this example shows that *a discard cannot win a trick.* (This implies that when you do have to discard, you should pick your most worthless card.)

Example 3: Notrump

SOUTH: Leads ♡ 6.	This time, South has the lead and elects to play the Six of Hearts.
WEST: Plays ♠ 9.	West has no Hearts, and discards the Nine of Spades.
NORTH: Plays ♣ A.	North is also out of Hearts, and unhappily discards the Ace of Clubs.
EAST: Plays ♢ 5.	East also has no Hearts, so he discards the Five of Diamonds. This time, however, he won't be very pleased with the result!

Result: South wins the trick, since his card was the highest one *of the suit led.* Although the cards are the same as in Example 2, the outcome is quite different because a different player was on lead. As you can see, even a meek and unassuming small card (like East's Five of Diamonds in Example 2, or South's Six of Hearts in Example 3) can on occasion turn into a powerful winner, provided that nobody else has any higher-ranking cards left in that suit (and that a trump doesn't appear on the scene) *and that its holder has the lead.*

Example 4: Hearts are trumps

NORTH:

Leads ♠ K.

In this example, North has the lead and plays the King of Spades.

EAST:

Plays ♠ 2.

East must follow suit if he can. He either doesn't have the Ace of Spades, or doesn't want to play it; and since no other Spade can possibly win this trick, he plays his smallest one.

SOUTH:

Plays ♣ 4.

South is out of Spades, and decides to discard the Four of Clubs; he does *not* have to play a trump if he doesn't want to. Apparently, he is hoping that his partner's high Spade will be good enough to win this trick, allowing him to save his trumps for later on (when North may be unable to help out). But . . .

WEST:

Plays ♡ 2.

West is also out of Spades, so he can play any card in his hand. He chooses to **trump (ruff)** by playing the Two of Hearts.

Result: West wins the trick, since *any* trump outranks any card of a different suit.

Example 5: Clubs are trumps

NORTH:
Leads ♠ K.

Once again, North is on lead and plays the King of Spades.

EAST:
Plays ♣ 5.

East has no Spades, so he tries to win the trick by trumping (ruffing) with the Five of Clubs. If no one else plays a higher trump (as will happen if they all can follow suit), he'll succeed. But...

SOUTH:
Plays ♣ 6.

South is also out of Spades, and **overtrumps** (**overruffs**) with the Six of Clubs.

WEST:
Plays ♠ 4.

West has some Spades, so he can't join in the ruffing action. Even the Ace of Spades can't win this trick now that a trump has appeared, so he gets rid of his smallest Spade.

Result: South wins the trick, because he played the *highest trump.* When more than one trump is played to a trick, the highest one is the winner.

When tricks should be won. One of the most unique and appealing aspects of bridge is that you will at times come out ahead by *not* winning a particular trick, even though you are fully able to do so. A great deal of strategy hinges on such factors as who has the lead, and whether or not to ruff:

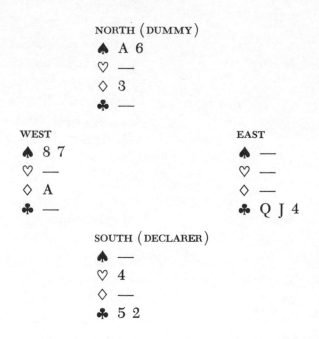

NORTH (DUMMY)
♠ A 6
♡ —
◇ 3
♣ —

WEST
♠ 8 7
♡ —
◇ A
♣ —

EAST
♠ —
♡ —
◇ —
♣ Q J 4

SOUTH (DECLARER)
♠ —
♡ 4
◇ —
♣ 5 2

For simplicity, we look in on a deal after ten tricks have taken place and each player has only three cards left. The dashes indicate that a player is out of (**void of**) that suit; thus, West and North have no Hearts or Clubs, South has no Spades or Diamonds, and East has only Clubs.

Hearts are trumps, and West has won the preceding

trick and therefore must lead to this one. He can see the Ace of Spades leering at him in the dummy, so he decides to seek his fortune elsewhere and leads the Ace of Diamonds. North has only one Diamond (a **singleton**) and so must play it; and East, observing that he is outgunned, looks around for his most worthless card and discards the Four of Clubs. As South, what card should you play from your hand to complete this trick? (In a real bridge game, of course, you could not see the East and West hands; but we will assume that you have keenly deduced the identity of their remaining cards.)

Since you cannot follow suit, you may play your trump (Four of Hearts) and capture this trick. But if you do, you must lead to the next trick; and unless you surreptitiously (and illegally) borrow a card from another deck, you'll have to play a Club. West and North will discard Spades, and East will happily rake in the trick with a high Club. He will then promptly lead out his other high Club, winning the last trick as well. As a result, your side will suffer the sad fate of watching dummy's Ace of Spades go down the drain! Since no one ever led a Spade (and since Spades were not trumps), the Ace never had a chance to be the highest card *of the suit led;* and, as we have seen, discards can't win tricks.

Can you somehow see to it that a Spade *is* led, so that dummy's Ace will become a winner? It looks difficult, since you don't have any Spades in your hand. (If you did, you could simply trump the Ace of Diamonds and lead a Spade yourself, playing dummy's Ace in due turn.) However, perhaps the (unwilling) aid of the enemy can be enlisted. Suppose you discard your Two of Clubs on West's

Ace of Diamonds, permitting him to win the first trick. He now has only Spades left *and is still on lead*, so you can be quite certain that a Spade will be led to the next trick. When it appears, you play dummy's Ace; and since this clinches the trick for your side, you discard the worthless Five of Clubs from your hand. Now your carefully preserved trump wins the last trick, and your side winds up with two tricks instead of just one.

As your bridge career progresses, you'll find many intriguing ways of quarterbacking a sequence of plays in order to produce the number of tricks that you need. But since you're probably wondering about such questions as how the trump suit is determined and who gets to be the declarer, let's return to our discussion of the rules of bridge.

The contract. The declarer's goal is to fulfill a promise, made during the bidding, to take a specified number of tricks; that is, he tries to **make his contract**. The other partnership, called the **defenders**, tries to frustrate him by taking enough tricks so that he winds up at least one short of his objective (is **set**, or **goes down**). To understand this aspect of bridge, however, it is necessary to take a closer look at the bidding phase of each deal.

THE ESSENTIALS OF BIDDING

GENERAL STRATEGY

Bridge offers substantial rewards for daring, provided that it is well-judged. If you *bid and make* a contract that requires a large number of tricks, you'll score a sizable profit. But if you bid for more tricks than you can take, you must pay a penalty; while if your side is overly timid, and you wind up taking many more tricks than you bid for, you'll have missed out on a chance for a windfall. Therefore, you must use the bidding to exchange information with your partner about your *ability to take tricks* (your **strength**), so that your side can accurately determine *how much* to bid.

As a further reward for valor, the side that is willing to risk the highest-level bid gets to name the trump suit (or Notrump). This means that you and your partner must also exchange information about your *long and short suits* (your **distribution**), so that your side can accurately determine *what* to bid. For example, suppose that six of your cards are Spades and four of them are Hearts, while your partner has four cards in Hearts and no Spades at all. If your partnership outbids the opponents and makes Hearts the trump suit, you'll have a real edge; the enemy will be outnumbered in the powerful trump department by 8 to 5. But if Spades should happen to wind up as the trump suit (either because your side blunders, or because you are so entranced with your own hand that you become a "bidding hog"), your delighted opponents will actually own more trumps than your team (7 to your 6). And if this sad fate should befall you, you won't be very happy with your result!

THE RULES OF BIDDING

Book. In order to bid at all, you must promise to take more than half the tricks. A bid of "one," therefore, actually promises to take *seven* of the 13 tricks on that deal; the first six tricks are called **book**, and do *not* count against the number mentioned in your bid. Tricks in excess of book are called **odd** tricks, so a one-bid pledges to take one odd trick (or "one-odd").

In addition to a number, a bid must also include one of the four suits or Notrump. Thus, an example of a legal bid would be "One Spade" (1 ♠). If you make this bid and it is followed by three consecutive passes, the auction will be over and you will be expected to take (at least) seven tricks with Spades as the trump suit (book of six, plus one extra or "odd" trick). If a bid of Three Notrump (3 NT) is followed by three consecutive passes, that partnership has promised to take (at least) nine tricks with no trump suit at all (book of six, plus three extra). And a bid of Seven Clubs (7 ♣) contracts to take all 13 tricks with Clubs as the trump suit (book plus seven old tricks). You are *not* allowed to bid more than seven, even though there are some rare situations where it would actually be to your advantage to do so, because it is physically impossible to take more than 13 tricks in any one deal.

Suit rank and bidding level. The dealer begins the auction, and he may bid anywhere from one to seven of any of the four suits or Notrump. If instead he is highly dubious about the trick-taking ability of his hand and does not wish to contest the issue (or encourage his partner to do so), he may pass. The bidding then proceeds clockwise around the table.

As in any auction, a player must *increase the previous bid* in order to get in on the action. This can be done *by bidding a higher-ranking denomination* than the preceding one, or *by offering to take more tricks*, or *both*. To illustrate, suppose that you are South. North deals and starts things off on a gloomy note by passing, and East elects to bid One Diamond (the **opening bid**, since it is the first call other than a pass). It is now your turn, and you must increase the auction if you wish to bid. You can do so by bidding One Heart, One Spade, or One Notrump, since Notrump and the major suits all outrank Diamonds. (Recall that the rank of the denominations during the auction, from highest to lowest, is: Notrump, Spades, Hearts, Diamonds, and Clubs.) But if you should want to bid Clubs, you must bid at least Two Clubs. Clubs are outranked by Diamonds, so a bid of One Club would *not* increase the auction (and would therefore be illegal or **insufficient**). The only way to make a higher bid in this situation is by promising to take more tricks than the previous bidder (increasing the **level** of bidding).

Here's an example of a complete auction, expressed in customary diagram form:

SOUTH (YOU)	WEST	NORTH	EAST
—	—	Pass	1 ◇
1 ♡	1 ♠	1 NT	2 ♣
Pass	Pass	2 ♡	Pass
Pass	Pass		

North deals and passes, East opens the bidding with One Diamond, and you (South) decide to bid One Heart. West gets into the act by bidding One Spade, which is legal since Spades is the highest-ranking suit. North now joins in by bidding One Notrump, taking advantage of the fact that Notrump outranks any suit. (North's original pass does *not* bar him from entering the auction later on; any player may bid when it is his turn to do so.)

East now wishes to mention the lowly Club suit, and must increase the level of bidding in order to do so. Both you and West have had enough; and if North now passes, the auction will be over and East and West will be expected to take eight tricks with Clubs as the trump suit. North is not about to surrender, though, and he fights on by bidding Two Hearts. This is followed by three consecutive passes, ending the auction, so you and your partner have pledged to take (at least) eight tricks with Hearts as the trump suit. Thus, Two Hearts becomes the contract. (The *last* bid is always the contract.)

Declarer and dummy. Since you were the *first* member of your team to bid the denomination *named in the contract*, Hearts, you become the declarer. The player to your left (West) makes the opening lead, and your partner (North) then becomes the dummy and places his entire hand face up on the table (as described previously).

Doubles and redoubles. If the most recent bid was made by an *opponent*, you are permitted to **double**; and if the enemy bid that you have doubled becomes the contract, the scoring will be substantially increased. But if a double is followed by some other bid, it is cancelled (since it no longer applies to the contract) and the scoring returns to normal. For example, suppose that you are South in the following auction:

SOUTH	WEST	NORTH	EAST
1 ♣	3 ♡	Double	3 ♠
?			

You deal and open the bidding with One Club, and West elects to bid Three Hearts (a **jump** bid, since One Heart would have been sufficient). The most recent bid has been made by an opponent, so North may double. If his double is followed by three consecutive passes, the contract will be *Three Hearts doubled,* and West will be the declarer in search of nine tricks with Hearts as trumps. If he makes his contract, he'll receive a sizable reward; but if he goes down, your team will collect an increased penalty.

East, however, fears that a doubled Heart contract will be a disaster for his side, so he bids Three Spades. (A double or redouble does *not* interfere with the normal order of bidding.) If this bid is followed by three passes in a row, the contract will be Three Spades *un*doubled (normal scoring). Alternatively, you may double Three Spades; or if you pass and West passes, North may double. But unless one of the opponents bids Hearts again, East's Three Spade bid will have ended your chances of playing a doubled Heart contract on this deal.

If the most recent call was a *double* by an *opponent,* you may **redouble**. If East had liked his side's chances to make Three Hearts, he might have chosen to redouble instead of bidding Three Spades; or, if East had passed and you also passed, West could redouble. If a redouble is followed by three consecutive passes, the scoring is increased still more; but if there is a subsequent bid, the redouble is cancelled and the scoring returns to normal. A redouble is the ultimate in increased scoring, so a bid that has been redoubled *cannot* be doubled any further.

Although the potential *effect* of a double or redouble is to increase the scoring, there are other *reasons* why you might wish to make one of these calls. Only fifteen words may legally be used during the bidding—the numbers one through seven, the four suits, Notrump, pass, double, and redouble. And because your choices are so limited, you will sometimes have to use a double or redouble *to convey information to your partner about your hand.*

HOW POINTS ARE WON

Making a Contract

If you are the declarer and take at least as many tricks as you bid for (make your contract), your partnership wins points for this accomplishment. The exact amount depends on the denomination that you have chosen:

DENOMINATION	POINTS FOR TRICKS ABOVE BOOK (ODD TRICKS)
Notrump	40 for first; 30 for each other
Major suit (♠ or ♡)	30 for each
Minor suit (◇ or ♣)	20 for each

The six tricks making up book do *not* earn any points. If you should bid One Spade and take seven tricks, your side receives 30 points (for the one trick *above book*); while if you bid Two Notrump and take eight tricks, your side collects 70 points (40 for the first odd trick and 30 for the second one).

DEFEATING A CONTRACT

If declarer fails to make his contract (is set, or goes down), his side scores nothing at all; and, to add insult to injury, his delighted opponents collect some points as a reward for defeating him (a **penalty**). For example, suppose an opponent bids Two Spades but takes only seven tricks. Since he has gone down, his partnership scores zero and your side receives a bonus. The more tricks declarer winds up short of his contract, the greater the amount of the penalty.*

GAMES AND RUBBERS

A single match or contest of bridge is called a *rubber*. To win a rubber, you must score two *games* before the opponents do; and if you are successful, your side receives a substantial bonus.

To make one game, you must *bid and make* a total of *100 points or more* before the opponents can do so. Game can be, and often is, made in a single deal. For example, suppose you bid Four Spades and take ten tricks. You have made your contract, so you score 30 points for every odd trick; and since you bid for four odd tricks, you receive 120 points towards game. Other ways of making game in a single deal (**game contracts**) are by bidding Four Hearts and taking at least ten tricks (120 points), bidding Three Notrump and taking at least nine tricks (100 points, or 40+30+30), or bidding Five Clubs or Five Diamonds and taking at least eleven tricks (100 points). Note that it is hardest to make game in Clubs or Diamonds, which is another reason why these suits are

* A complete scoring table is provided in the Appendix.

accorded the inferior title of "minors." And Notrump, in addition to being the highest-ranking denomination, requires the fewest tricks for game.

Game can also be made by stringing together two or more smaller contracts (**part-scores**, or **partials**) that add up to 100 points or more, *provided that you do so before the opponents score game first.* For example, suppose you bid only Two Spades and make ten tricks (possibly because you undervalued your assets, perhaps because your opponents did not defend as well as they might have). Only tricks *bid for and made* count towards game, so your 120-point award is split into two parts: 60 points count towards game (30 for each of the two odd tricks *that you bid for*), while the other 60 points do not. You can now complete the game by bidding and making a contract that pays 40 points or more (such as One Notrump or two of any suit), or even by bidding and making One Club on each of the next two deals. But if your opponents beat you to the punch by making game themselves, you lose your advantage; your part-score is "wiped out," and you must start from zero in the battle for the next game. Therefore, *it's very desirable to bid game when you have enough strength to make it.*

You cannot make more than one game on a single deal. Even if you bid and make Seven Hearts (210 points), you get credit for only one game (and must start the next one from zero). However, an enemy blunder may sometimes let you score a game with a low bid. Suppose you bid Two Hearts, the opponents double, and you take eight tricks. Since you have made a doubled contract, you *double* the score for *the odd tricks you bid for;* and since twice 60 is equal to 120, you have made a game! And if you should happen to make One Spade *redoubled*, you'll actually score a game for taking just seven tricks (since 30 doubled and doubled again equals 120).

SLAMS

The **slam** adds a particularly exciting dimension to the game of bridge. If you *bid for and make twelve tricks*, you have made a **small slam** and receive a substantial bonus; while if you *bid for and make all thirteen tricks*, this crowning achievement is called a **grand slam** and earns an even larger bonus. And making slam also means that you have made a game, since slam contracts are worth more than 100 points.

Although slams are very lucrative, they are high risk propositions. If you bid a small slam and take only eleven tricks, you score nothing at all (and the opponents collect a penalty) because you failed to make your contract. Had you stopped at the five-level and taken the same eleven tricks, you would have made a game! And bidding a grand slam and taking only twelve tricks is a real catastrophe, for you'll have blown a small slam. Therefore, going down in slam costs you much more than the penalty you pay out to the opponents; *you also lose the game or small slam that you would have scored by being more conservative*. This makes slam bidding one of the most challenging aspects in all of bridge.

HOW TO KEEP SCORE

Since you're undoubtedly eager to begin playing bridge, a full discussion of scoring will be reserved for the Appendix. A certain degree of familiarity with scoring is essential, however, so let's look at a few examples. A standard bridge score sheet look like this:

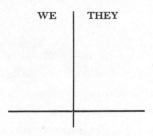

WE | THEY

Points towards game (for tricks bid for and made) go *below* the horizontal line; *all* other points go *above* the line. To illustrate, suppose your opponents bid Two Clubs and take eleven tricks. Insofar as game is concerned, they receive only 40 points (20 for each of the two odd tricks that they bid for), and this score is placed below the line. They also receive a total of 60 points for the three extra tricks that they didn't bid for (**overtricks**), and this score goes above the line:

WE | THEY

	60
	40

On the next deal, your side bids Three Notrump and makes nine tricks. Since you cleverly bid for all of the three odd tricks that you made, all 100 points go below the line. Thus you have won the race for the first game, and the score sheet now looks like this:

WE	THEY
	60
100	40

A new horizontal line is drawn to indicate that the first game is over, and each side must start from zero in the fight to win the second game. Let's suppose that on the next deal, the opponents bid One Notrump and take eight tricks; while on the following deal, your side bids Four Spades and takes ten tricks. Your side has won two games, so you have *won the rubber*. To see how much this triumph is actually worth, let's examine the final score sheet:

WE	THEY
	30
700	60
100	40
120	40

The double horizontal line indicates that the rubber is over. Winning it by 2 games to 0 earns a 700-point bonus, while winning by 2 games to 1 would be worth 500 points. The total for your side is 920 points and the enemy has scored 170 points, so your side has won 750 points. If the opponents want a rematch, you start the next rubber 750 points ahead; while if partnerships are switched, a separate score (**back score**) is kept with everyone's name, the two winners receive +750, and the two losers receive —750.*

---

* Many bridge players like to round scores off to the nearest hundred for convenience. Scores ending in 50 are rounded up, so this result would be entered as +8 and —8 on the back score.

Before leaving the topic of scoring, two important points must be noted. First, the penalties for going down are greater when your team has scored one game (is **vulnerable**) and smaller when you don't have a game (are **not vulnerable**). This suggests that caution is more desirable when you are vulnerable; but it is a mistake to be too timid, for the bonus for making a slam is greater if you are vulnerable. Second, there is a special bonus of 100 points for holding four *trump* honors (A K Q J, A K Q 10, or K Q J 10) *in one hand* (**100 honors**). If one player is lucky enough to hold all five *trump* honors (A K Q J 10), or *all four aces at a Notrump contract*, his side receives a 150-point bonus (**150 honors**). This bonus must be claimed by calling it to the attention of the opponents *before the next deal begins*; but you can (and should) wait until the end of the deal before announcing honors, so that the opponents won't be able to profit from a knowledge of your cards during the play.

THE PROPRIETIES

Experienced bridge players will make allowances for your mistakes, but bad bridge manners are another story. During a bridge game, you must be careful to communicate with your partner *only through the actual calls and plays that you make*, and *not* by the *way* you make them. In particular:

Don't invent new wording during the bidding (such as "I double Three Diamonds," "I'll bid One Club," or even "A Club"); use proper bidding language (such as "double" or "One Club").

Don't bid loudly or quickly to show a strong hand, and softly or slowly to show a weak one.

Don't play unusually quickly to show that you have no problem.

Don't play unusually slowly when you have no problem in order to fool the opponents.

Don't detach a card from your hand before it is your turn to play (thereby indicating that you have no problem).

Don't slam or snap your cards on the table during the play because you are triumphant or angry.

Don't make idle comments that may help your partner or mislead the opponents.

Don't take advantage of any improper information that your partner may happen to send; force yourself to forget it.

Do be a player who takes the proprieties seriously, so that you'll be welcome in any bridge game!

BRIDGE MOVIE 1:
AN INTRODUCTION TO BRIDGE

At various points in this book, you'll find a special feature called Bridge Movies that will actually enable you to play bridge all by yourself. Cover this page with a sheet of paper and slide the paper down slowly until you reach the first question, which will be in *italics*. (Be careful not to expose the answer that follows.) Stop, decide on your solution, and then move the paper down to reveal the answer and the next question. Continue in this fashion until you have bid and played the entire deal.

♠ ♡ ◇ ♣

You and three friends get together for an evening of bridge, and you decide to cut for partners. The results are:

You: ♡ 8	Player Y: ♣ A
Player X: ♠ 5	Player Z: ◇ 8

What are the partnerships, and who is the first dealer?

ANSWER: You and Player Y are partners, because you drew the two highest cards. (Hearts outrank Diamonds, so your Eight-spot is higher than Player Z's for purposes of this cut.) Thus, Player X and Player Z are also partners. And your partner, who drew the highest card of all, is the first dealer.

For ease of reference, let's suppose that you are South. Your partner, North, now shuffles the deck thoroughly. *Who cuts the deck? And who is dealt the first card?*

ANSWER: West, the player to the dealer's right, cuts the deck. North then deals the first card (face down) to the player at his left (East), deals the second card to you, and continues clockwise around the table until the entire deck has been distributed.

You pick up and sort your hand, which is:

♠ A 10 5 3 2
♡ J 6
◇ K 4 2
♣ 8 6 5

Who starts the auction, and what calls is that player allowed to make?

ANSWER: The dealer, North, begins the auction. He may bid from one to seven of any of the four suits or Notrump, or he may pass. In fact, the only things he can't do are double and redouble.

North elects to open the bidding with One Club. *Who is next, and what calls can he legally make?*

ANSWER: The auction proceeds clockwise, so the player on your right (East) is next to speak. He may bid One Diamond, One Heart, One Spade, One Notrump, or from two to seven of any suit or Notrump; or he may double; or he may pass.

NORTH	EAST
1 ♣	1 ♡

East decides to bid One Heart. *Who is next, and what calls are legal?*

ANSWER: It is your turn. You may bid One Spade or One Notrump, or from two to seven of any suit or Notrump; or you may double; or you may pass. But you cannot bid One Club, One Diamond, or One Heart, since these bids wouldn't increase the auction.

SOUTH	WEST	NORTH	EAST
—	—	1 ♣	1 ♡
1 ♠	Pass	4 ♠	Pass
Pass	Pass		

You choose to bid One Spade. West passes, and North makes a jump bid of Four Spades. East, you, and West all pass.

Could North have doubled instead of bidding Four Spades? And could West have bid over Four Spades?

ANSWER: North was not allowed to double at his second turn, since the most recent bid was made by his partner. West, however, could have bid over Four Spades if he wished; he was not barred by his previous pass. However, he would have had to bid Four Notrump or five, six, or seven of any suit or Notrump in order to outbid North.

Who makes the next call?

ANSWER: Nobody! Since there have been three consecutive passes, the auction is over.

What is the contract, who is the declarer, who is the

dummy, and who makes the opening lead?

ANSWER: The contract is Four Spades, and your side will be expected to take (at least) ten tricks with Spades as the trump suit. Since you were the first player on your team to bid the denomination named in the contract (Spades), you are the declarer and will have the fun of handling all the plays for your team. Your partner, North, is the dummy; and West, the player to the declarer's left, makes the opening lead.

Exactly what happens now?

ANSWER: West selects any card from his hand and places it face up in the center of the table. After he has done so, North places his entire hand face up on the table in four columns, one for each suit. The trump suit, Spades, should be at your extreme left, and the suits should alternate in color.

West leads the Four of Hearts, and the dummy is as follows (with your hand repeated for convenience):

NORTH (DUMMY)

♠ K Q J 4
♡ 9 5 2
◇ A 10
♣ A K Q 2

Since the actual appearance of this dummy was shown earlier in this chapter, it is presented here in customary diagram form.

Opening
Lead: ♡ 4

SOUTH (DECLARER)

♠ A 10 5 3 2
♡ J 6
◇ K 4 2
♣ 8 6 5

What are the only legal plays at this point?

ANSWER: The Two of Hearts, the Five of Hearts, and the Nine of Hearts. Play always proceeds clockwise around the table, so you must play a card from dummy; and you must follow suit if you are able to do so.

You decide to play the Two of Hearts, so you remove it from the dummy and place it in the center of the table. *What happens now?*

ANSWER: It is East's turn to play a card, and he must also follow suit if he can. (And he should be able to, since he bid Hearts!)

East plays the Queen of Hearts. *Who is next, and what is that player allowed to do?*

ANSWER: It's your turn to complete the trick by playing a card from your hand, and you are required to choose one of your Hearts.

Since you can't beat East's Queen, your side can't win this trick. Therefore, you play your smallest Heart, the Six-spot.

What happens to this trick now that it is completed, and who plays first to the next one?

ANSWER: Either East or West gathers in the four cards, groups them into a single neat packet, and places the trick face down off to one side where it won't be in the way. Then East, who won the trick, leads to the next one by choosing any card in his hand and placing it face up in the center of the table.

NORTH (DUMMY)

♠ K Q J 4
♡ 9 5
♢ A 10
♣ A K Q 2

East elects to lead the King of Hearts, and the current situation is shown at the left.

Lead: ♡ K

SOUTH (DECLARER)

♠ A 10 5 3 2
♡ J
♢ K 4 2
♣ 8 6 5

Who plays next, and which side is going to win this trick?

ANSWER: You must play a card from your hand, and you have no choice; you have to follow suit by playing your only remaining Heart, the Jack. And since dummy is also unable to beat East's King, the opponents are sure to win this trick regardless of what West does.

West actually plays the Eight of Hearts, and you select dummy's Five of Hearts. The trick is now complete, and is gathered in by the opponent who collected the preceding trick.

NORTH (DUMMY)

♠ K Q J 4
♡ 9
◇ A 10
♣ A K Q 2

East still has the lead, since his King of Hearts won the last trick. He now plays the Ace of Hearts.

Lead: ♡ A

SOUTH (DECLARER)

♠ A 10 5 3 2
♡ —
◇ K 4 2
♣ 8 6 5

What do you play?

ANSWER: A Spade, preferably the Ten (or Ace). Since you are unable to follow suit, you may play any card in your hand. Dummy is going to have to play the Nine of Hearts when its turn arrives, so discarding a Club or Diamond will lose the trick for your side. Fortunately, you can prevent this calamity by playing a trump, which outranks any card of any other suit. And since you have so many high Spades, you might as well guard against the possibility that West is also out of Hearts. If he is, and if you ruff with the Two of Spades, he can foil you by playing a higher trump (overtrumping, or overruffing).

You ruff with the Ten of Spades, West plays the Ten of Hearts (so your trumping high turns out to be unnecessary), and dummy's Nine of Hearts completes the trick. *After you have gathered it in, who leads to the next trick?*

ANSWER: You must lead a card from your hand (South), since that is where you won the preceding trick.

NORTH (DUMMY)

♠ K Q J 4
♡ —
◇ A 10
♣ A K Q 2

SOUTH (DECLARER)

♠ A 5 3 2
♡ —
◇ K 4 2
♣ 8 6 5

You decide to lead the Two of Spades. West plays the Seven of Spades, you put on dummy's King of Spades (the Queen or Jack would be equally correct), and East contributes the Six of Spades. Dummy's card wins the trick (as you knew it must, since you have the only higher Spade in your hand), so you gather it in. Dummy now has the lead, and you select the Queen of Spades. East plays the Eight of Spades, you play the

Three of Spades, and West
discards the Three of Diamonds.

*Who wins this trick? What does West's play tell you
about his hand, and about East's hand?*

ANSWER: Dummy's Queen of Spades wins the trick.
West's card was neither the highest card of the suit led
nor a trump, so it has no bearing on the outcome. And
since he did not follow suit, his play also reveals that he
must be out of Spades.

This situation illustrates how a sharp declarer can make
important deductions about the unseen enemy hands.
Your side started with nine cards in Spades (five in your
hand, and four in the dummy). Each opponent played a
Spade on the first round of the suit, accounting for two
more, and one of them played a Spade to the next trick.
Thus, a total of 12 Spades have appeared; and since there
are 13 Spades in every deck, the enemy has one Spade left.
And since West's discard is proof that he is fresh out of
Spades, you can be absolutely certain that East has it!

NORTH (DUMMY)

♠ J 4
♡ —
◊ A 10
♣ A K Q 2

SOUTH (DECLARER)

♠ A 5
♡ —
◊ K 4 2
♣ 8 6 5

You now decide to get rid of the last enemy trump before it can do any damage (such as ruffing away one of your side's Aces or Kings). The lead is in dummy, and let's suppose that you pick the Jack of Spades (equal to the Ace at this point, since the King and Queen of Spades have been played). East plays the Nine of Spades, you play your Five of Spades, and West discards the Five of Diamonds.

Next, you elect to lead dummy's Ace of Diamonds. East plays the Seven of Diamonds, you play the Two of Diamonds, and West follows with the Six of Diamonds.

NORTH (DUMMY)

♠ 4
♡ —
◊ 10
♣ A K Q 2

You now lead dummy's Ten of Diamonds, and East follows with the Nine of Diamonds.

SOUTH (DECLARER)

♠ A
♡ —
◊ K 4
♣ 8 6 5

What card do you play from your hand?

ANSWER: The King of Diamonds. If you play the Four-spot, you are very likely to lose the trick; the Queen and Jack of Diamonds have not yet appeared, so West could easily be able to beat dummy's Ten. And there is no reason to take this risk, since you can take all the rest of the tricks if you play correctly.

West follows with the Eight of Diamonds. You gather in yet another trick, and the lead is now in your hand in this position:

NORTH (DUMMY)

♠ 4
♡ —
◇ —
♣ A K Q 2

You lead the Four of Diamonds, and West plays the Jack of Diamonds.

SOUTH (DECLARER)

♠ A
♡
◇ 4
♣ 8 6 5

What do you play from dummy?

ANSWER: The Four of Spades. Dummy is out of the suit that has been led and therefore may play any card, so you can—and should—overcome the enemy's superior Diamond power by trumping this trick.

The rest of the tricks are easily yours. You lead out one of dummy's Club honors (let's say the Ace) to the next trick, lead the King of Clubs to the subsequent trick, and lead the Queen of Clubs to the trick after that (being careful to follow suit from your hand each time). The opponents are helpless against this impressive display of power! This highest Club they own is the Jack, which can't beat any of dummy's honors, and they are out of trumps. Thus, so long as you are careful to avoid the serious blunder of leading the Two of Clubs to one of these tricks, there is no conceivable way that the opponents can win any of them. Finally, the trump in your hand captures the last trick, and the deal has come to an end.

Did you make your contract?

ANSWER: You certainly did. Your Four Spade contract pledged to take at least ten tricks with Spades as the trump suit, and you actually took eleven—all except the first two.

Did you make a game?

ANSWER: Yes. Tricks bid for and made count towards game and Spades pays off at 30 points per trick, so bidding and making Four Spades is worth 120 points—more than the minimum of 100 required for game.

Did you lose anything by not bidding Five Spades, since you did in fact take eleven tricks?

ANSWER: Nothing at all. You still get 30 points for the extra trick (overtrick). The only penalty is that these points don't count towards game, which doesn't matter since you made a game anyway. And Five Spades is not a slam contract, so there was nothing more to be gained by bidding it.

The only times when you should wind up in a contract like Five Spades, which is more than you need for game but not enough for slam, are when : (1) The opponents force you to go that high in order to outbid them (for example, they bid Five Hearts), or (2) You think that you have a chance for slam and bid past game in order to exchange information, and then decide that slam is out of reach and you had better stop while there is still time.

What does the score sheet look like at this point?

ANSWER: Like this:

WE	THEY
30	
120	

Since we have covered a lot of ground in this Bridge Movie, you may wish to get a deck of cards and replay the action. Here's the complete deal:

NORTH
♠ K Q J 4
♡ 9 5 2
◇ A 10
♣ A K Q 2

WEST
♠ 7
♡ 10 8 4
◇ J 8 6 5 3
♣ J 10 9 7

EAST
♠ 9 8 6
♡ A K Q 7 3
◇ Q 9 7
♣ 4 3

SOUTH
♠ A 10 5 3 2
♡ J 6
◇ K 4 2
♣ 8 6 5

The bidding:

SOUTH	WEST	NORTH	EAST
—	—	1 ♣	1 ♡
1 ♠	Pass	4 ♠	Pass
Pass	Pass		

Basic Bidding and Play

Each deal of bridge is a battle for tricks, with declarer trying to make his contract and the defenders fighting to stop him. Therefore, it's essential to understand the different ways in which tricks can be won. They are:

1. Power—playing high cards that the opponents can't beat. Example: You hold the A K Q of Clubs. You lead out your honors, and win three tricks because the opponents don't own any higher Clubs.

2. Promotion—turning lesser cards into winners by driving out the higher ones. Example: Your Diamond holding is K Q J and partner has 7 4 3. You lead one of your honors and the opponents take their Ace, whereupon your remaining honors become high and win the next two Diamond tricks.

3. Finesse—taking tricks with cards that are smaller than ones still held by the opponents. Example: Your Heart holding is A Q and partner has 5 2. You can't afford to lead out your honors, since the opponents will play small on your Ace and grab the Queen with their King; but if you play skillfully *and if you are lucky*, you may be able to frustrate the enemy King and snag a second trick with the Queen.

4. **Trumps—beating enemy high cards by ruffing.** Example: Partner has a few small cards in a non-trump suit (**side suit**), and you are void of this suit and have some trumps. Partner leads one of his low cards and the opponents hopefully play higher ones, but you win the trick by ruffing it.

5. **Length—turning small cards into winners by exhausting the enemy of that suit.** Example: Your Spade holding is 6 5 4 3 2 and partner has 9 8 7. You manage to gain the lead on three separate occasions, and play a Spade each time. These tricks are won by the opponents; but, as it happens, they use up all their Spades in the process. You now regain the lead and play Spades, and win two tricks because nobody else is able to follow suit.

Let's take a closer look at each of these intriguing and important methods.

WINNING TRICKS WITH HIGH CARDS

POWER

On some occasions, power will be all you need for victory. If your opponents should blunder into Six Notrump when you are the opening leader and hold the Ace and King of the same suit, you can quickly defeat their slam contract by leading out your top honors. Or:

WEST	EAST
♠ A 7 3	♠ 6 4 2
♡ K 4 3	♡ A 8 5
◇ K 6 5	◇ A 9 4
♣ A K 8 2	♣ Q J 7 6

You are West, and North leads the King of Spades against your Three Notrump contract. You need nine tricks, and you can rattle them off quite easily no matter how the enemy cards are distributed. Just be sure to play an honor from one hand to each of the first nine tricks, following suit with a small card from the other hand. For example, it doesn't matter whether you tackle the Club suit by leading the Ace from your hand and playing the Six-spot from dummy, or by leading the deuce and playing dummy's Jack; since the highest Club owned by the enemy is the Ten, any one of your side's honors must win the trick to which it is played. So long as you avoid the egregious mistake of wasting two high honors on the same trick, you're certain to wind up with four Club tricks, two Diamond tricks, two Heart tricks, and one Spade trick— and your game contract.

Entries. At times, getting the most out of your side's power will require careful forethought:

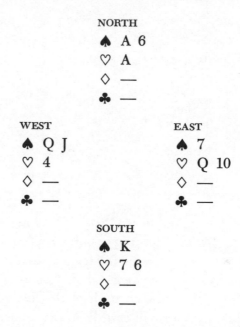

NORTH
♠ A 6
♡ A
♢ —
♣ —

WEST
♠ Q J
♡ 4
♢ —
♣ —

EAST
♠ 7
♡ Q 10
♢ —
♣ —

SOUTH
♠ K
♡ 7 6
♢ —
♣ —

We join this deal at a crucial moment: South needs to win all of these last three tricks to make his Notrump contract, and the lead is in his own hand. As South, how do you plan the play?

If you lead a Heart, you'll soon be in serious trouble! Dummy's Ace will win the trick, but you'll then be reduced to the following sad choice:

Disaster 1. You can now lead dummy's Six of Spades and win the trick with your King, get stuck in your hand, and have to lead a Heart to the last trick. East will gleefully win it with the Queen of Hearts (highest card of the suit led!) while you unhappily *discard* dummy's Ace of Spades.

Disaster 2. Alternatively, you can now lead dummy's

Ace of Spades and watch your King self-destruct on the same trick (you must follow suit!). West now wins the last trick with the Queen of Spades.

Planning before playing will keep you unstuck. Start off by leading the King of Spades, playing the Six-spot from dummy. *Now* lead a Heart to the Ace. This enables you to *lead* dummy's Spade Ace, so you win the last trick as well. (In bridge terminology, the Ace of Hearts is called an **entry** to dummy.) The same strategy will also work if the lead happens to be in dummy at the outset; lead the Six of Spades to your King, enter dummy by leading a Heart, and then cash the Ace of Spades.

Here's another example:

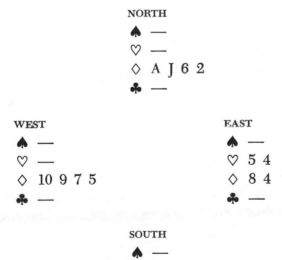

NORTH
♠ —
♡ —
◇ A J 6 2
♣ —

WEST
♠ —
♡ —
◇ 10 9 7 5
♣ —

EAST
♠ —
♡ 5 4
◇ 8 4
♣ —

SOUTH
♠ —
♡ 2
◇ K Q 3
♣ —

Once again, South has the lead in a Notrump contract and desperately needs to win all of the remaining tricks. As South, how should you proceed?

The right technique is to lead the King and Queen of Diamonds to the first two tricks, playing small from dummy each time. Now lead the Three of Diamonds and play one of dummy's honors, giving dummy the lead so that you can cash the remaining honor. Any other plan will fare more poorly; if you should lead your Three of Diamonds to the first trick, or if you overtake one of your honors with dummy's Ace, you'll eventually wind up with only three tricks instead of four.

Duplication of values. Although high honors are valuable assets, they don't always pull their full weight:

NORTH

◇ A J

SOUTH

◇ K Q

Here, both you and your partner must play a Diamond honor to each of the first two tricks; and this bridge disaster, which is known as **duplication of values**, will limit your side to just two winners.* Note that in the preceding example, North's lowly Six and Two of Diamonds and your own Three-spot actually increase your trick-taking power in Diamonds by two full tricks! One of the most

---

* This implies that if you should urgently need an entry to dummy, you have nothing to lose by overtaking your King or Queen with dummy's Ace. You'll eventually have to do it anyway!

appealing aspects of bridge is that even very low cards can at times be jewels of the highest value.

PROMOTION

Most of the time, power won't produce enough winners to make or defeat a contract. Fortunately, you'll often be able to **promote** lower honors into full-fledged winners by driving out the higher cards in that suit, *provided that you save your top honors in other suits until you have developed the total number of tricks that you need*:

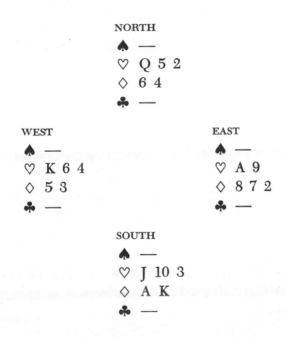

NORTH
♠ —
♡ Q 5 2
◇ 6 4
♣ —

WEST
♠ —
♡ K 6 4
◇ 5 3
♣ —

EAST
♠ —
♡ A 9
◇ 8 7 2
♣ —

SOUTH
♠ —
♡ J 10 3
◇ A K
♣ —

You are South and the lead is in your hand, and you need *three* of these last five tricks to make your Notrump contract. What is your plan?

You can grab two tricks in a hurry by leading out your power winners in Diamonds, but this faux pas will cost you your contract. You'll then have to lead a Heart, and let's say that West wins this trick with the King and leads another Heart. East wins with the Ace, so dummy's Queen is now high—but it won't do you any good! East fires back a *Diamond* to the last trick, and you can't contest the issue because your side is fresh out of this suit. Instead, you and dummy must discard your Hearts, and East's measly Eight-spot wins the last trick (length winner!).

This gross injustice can be avoided by promoting a trick in Hearts *before* your Diamond honors are driven from the field of battle. Start off by leading a Heart (let's say the Jack). Suppose West wins with the King and returns a Diamond. You win with one of your honors and lead the Ten of Hearts, playing small from dummy, and East takes his Ace and leads another Diamond. You capture this with your remaining Diamond honor and lead a Heart to the last trick, and dummy's Queen provides the third winner that you need to make your contract. (You could, of course, lead the Three of Hearts at the beginning and put up dummy's Queen if West played low; just be sure to play a high enough Heart to each trick to force out an enemy honor.)

A defender may also snatch defeat from the jaws of victory by cashing a top honor too soon:

NORTH (DUMMY)
♠ A
♡ —
◇ K 3
♣ —

WEST
♠ 6
♡ —
◇ 8 6
♣ —

EAST (YOU)
♠ 2
♡ —
◇ A 2
♣ —

SOUTH (DECLARER)
♠ 8
♡ —
◇ 5 4
♣ —

You are East and have the lead, and declarer needs to win two of the last three tricks to make the contract. If you succumb to the temptation of leading your Ace, he'll succeed! Keenly observing that his side is outgunned on this trick, he'll deposit dummy's Three of Diamonds on your Ace. The King of Diamonds will now be promoted to top rank, and dummy's high cards will easily win the last two tricks.

A better plan is to lead your Spade. Dummy must win with the Ace, and you are now in command: If the King of Diamonds is led, you pounce on it with your Ace, and partner's Eight-spot wins the last trick. And if instead dummy leads the Diamond Three, you play your deuce and let partner win the trick. He now returns the favor by leading his remaining Diamond, enabling you to capture dummy's King with your Ace and win a second trick for your side. Moral: Be careful not to promote tricks for the enemy by leading out your power winners too soon!

FINESSES

How to finesse. In the previous examples, your partnership held an unbroken sequence of honors such as A K Q J or Q J 10. Therefore, it didn't matter which hand led to the trick. When your side has honors that are *not* in sequence, however, careful handling and good luck will be required in order to build additional tricks:

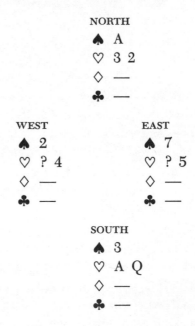

NORTH
♠ A
♡ 3 2
◇ —
♣ —

WEST
♠ 2
♡ ? 4
◇ —
♣ —

EAST
♠ 7
♡ ? 5
◇ —
♣ —

SOUTH
♠ 3
♡ A Q
◇ —
♣ —

You are South, the lead is in your hand, and you don't

know which one of your wily opponents has the King of Hearts. Is there any way to win three tricks?

Leading the Ace of Hearts won't work, for the opponents will simply play low and then take the Queen with their King. Leading the Queen will also result in certain defeat. But observe what happens if you enter dummy by leading a Spade to the Ace and then *lead a Heart from dummy.* This clever scheme *forces East to commit himself before you do,* and one of two good things may happen:

1. East has the King, and decides to play it. You top it with your Ace, promoting your Queen into a winner.

2. East has the King, but elects to play his Five-spot. You now *play your Queen* (a **finesse**, since you are trying to win a trick with a card that is lower than one still held by the enemy). East is strictly debarred from changing his play and West can't beat the Queen, so you win the trick.

If West has the King of Hearts, he'll capture your Queen and win the first trick. But if this is the case, there is no way to win more than one Heart trick; and since West must now lead a card that you can win, no damage is done and you still get the two tricks to which you were always entitled.

Here are some other card combinations that may produce extra tricks if you are lucky—and if you play correctly. In each case, you are declaring the contract from the South chair and North is the dummy; and there are several entries to each hand in different suits, so you can arrange to lead from whichever hand you prefer.

(a) NORTH   (b) NORTH   (c) NORTH
    ♡ K 3   ♠ Q 6 2   ◇ K 3 2

    SOUTH   SOUTH   SOUTH
    ♡ 7 4   ♠ A 7 3   ◇ A J 4

Your only chance to win one trick in example (a) is by making good use of dummy's King, so you can't afford to let the opponents Ace it. Therefore, lead a Heart from your hand and hope that West has the Ace. If he plays it, follow with the Three-spot and win the next Heart trick with the King; while if he plays low, put up the King.

In example (b), cash the Ace and lead a small Spade from your hand. This will produce a second trick any time West has the King, since he'll have to commit himself before dummy does. Leading the Queen won't work, since either opponent can easily prevent it from taking a trick by covering it with the King.*

The best plan in example (c) is to cash the King and lead a small Diamond from dummy, intending to finesse the Jack if East plays low. This produces three tricks whenever East has the Queen, whereas cashing the top honors will yield an extra trick only if the Queen is singleton or accompanied by just one small card (**doubleton**). Unless you have some overwhelming reason to

---

* If there is a *very* good reason to believe that East has the King (for example, he may have bid strongly), you do have one desperate chance. After cashing the Ace, play a small Spade for both hands! If East began with no more than two Spades, his King will come tumbling down—and dummy's Queen will become a winner.

believe that West has the Queen, therefore, the finesse is the superior play.

(d) NORTH
♣ Q 3 2

SOUTH
♣ A J 4

(e) NORTH
♣ 5 4 2

SOUTH
♣ A Q J

(f) NORTH
♣ A J 4

SOUTH
♣ Q 10 3

Case (d) is similar to (c); lead a small Club from dummy and finesse the Jack if East plays low. If this wins, cash the Ace of Clubs. This method produces three tricks if East happened to begin with the singleton or doubleton King; while if you start by leading dummy's Queen, the opponents can always limit you to two tricks by covering with the King.

Although the honors in example (e) are identical, you actually have a much better chance to win three tricks because their location is superior. Begin by leading a small Club from dummy, finessing the Queen (or Jack) if East plays low. If the finesse wins, reenter dummy in a different suit and repeat it.

In case (f), the addition of the Ten makes up for the fact that the honors are divided between the two hands. The right strategy is to lead the Queen (or Ten) from your hand, and take the finesse if West plays small. If it wins, you can promptly repeat it because the lead remains in your hand. And you don't mind if West covers the Queen with the King in this situation, for the Jack and Ten will take excellent care of the two remaining tricks.

(g) NORTH   (h) NORTH   (i) NORTH
  ♣ A 4 3   ◊ J 10 3   ♡ A J 3

SOUTH   SOUTH   SOUTH
  ♣ Q J 2   ◊ A K 6   ♡ K 10 7

If you need three tricks in example (g), you're in terrible trouble! The only chance is to play the Ace and pray that the King drops singleton, which is almost a 100-to-1 shot. When you need just two winners from this combination, however, it might well be a shrewd idea to lead the Queen for a finesse. If West has the King, you win two tricks without allowing the opponents to gain the lead and start an attack of their own; and even if East turns up with the King, you'll still have two winners because your Ace and Jack will be high.

In case (h), start by cashing the Ace of Diamonds. This will avoid defeat (and humiliation!) if West happens to have the singleton Queen. Then enter dummy in a different suit, and lead the Jack for a finesse. East is welcome to cover with the Queen if he wishes, for dummy's Ten will then control the third round of Diamonds.

In example (i), you can finesse either opponent for the Queen! If you think East has it, cash the Ace, lead the next round from dummy, and take the finesse if East plays low. But if you think the Queen resides with West, cash the King and lead small to dummy's Jack. Your decision about this **two-way finesse** may be influenced by the bidding, since an opponent who bids strongly is more likely to have the missing honor. Or your choice may be affected by the preceding play, since an opponent who has shown up with great length in several other suits won't have much room left in his hand for the Queen of Hearts. In the absence of such clues (and of ESP), you must guess what to do.

The double finesse. Suppose that your partnership owns either of these Heart holdings:

(j) NORTH
♡ 4 3 2

SOUTH
♡ A J 10

(k) NORTH
♡ A Q 10

SOUTH
♡ 7 6 4

In example (j), you have a very fine chance to win two tricks, provided that you begin by leading a small Heart from dummy. If East plays the Queen or King, win with the Ace and drive out the remaining honor by leading Hearts from your hand; while if East plays low, finesse the Jack (or Ten). If this loses, enter dummy when you regain the lead and finesse against the remaining enemy honor. This procedure, which is called a **double finesse** because it is executed against *two* higher cards, fails only if West has both the King and Queen.

In case (k), lead a small Heart from your hand and finesse the Ten if West plays low. If it wins, reenter your hand in a different suit and then finesse the Queen. This line wins all three tricks whenever West has both the King and Jack. However, you can't afford to reverse the order of these plays. If you begin by finessing the Queen, West will retain the K J against dummy's A 10 and will have to win one trick. Therefore, the immediate finesse of the Queen is correct only if you need precisely two tricks and cannot afford to lose the lead.

Help from the enemy. Some finesse positions require the aid of the opponents:

(1) NORTH	(m) NORTH
♠ Q 6	♡ A Q 5
SOUTH	SOUTH
♠ A 4	♡ 10 4 3

There is no good way to handle example (1). Leading the Ace of Spades leaves dummy's Queen embarrassingly bare, so it will surely fall victim to the King on the next Spade trick. Leading small from your hand won't gain even if West has the King, for he will play it and your honors will collide on the next trick. And leading dummy's Queen won't help even if East has the King, so long as he is clever enough to cover.

In this dire situation, the only chance for two tricks (save for a wildly unlikely singleton King) is to persuade the opponent with the King to lead the suit. If West leads a Spade, put up dummy's Queen and hope that East can't top it; while if East leads a Spade, play low from your hand and hope that West is unable to produce the King. But be careful not to confuse this case with example (b), where you had an additional Spade in each hand. If West leads a Spade in that situation, you should play low from dummy unless you are in a great hurry for two tricks. Thanks to the extra Spade, this *won't* leave your Queen all alone; and East will now be in serious trouble if he has the King and gains the lead in a different suit, since playing Spades will force him to commit himself before dummy and allow the Queen to become a winner.

If West leads a low Heart in example (m), play small from dummy. This will produce three tricks if West began with K J, since you'll win with the Ten and then finesse the Queen. And you'll create a second winner if West began with just the Jack, for East will have to put up the King to win the trick and your Ace and Queen will become high. Tackling the suit by yourself will produce one less trick in each case.

When not to finesse. The following layout may appear similar to the one that introduced the finesse, but it is actually fraught with far greater danger:

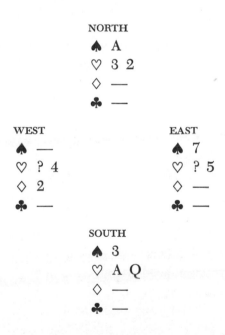

NORTH
♠ A
♡ 3 2
♢ —
♣ —

WEST
♠ —
♡ ? 4
♢ 2
♣ —

EAST
♠ 7
♡ ? 5
♢ —
♣ —

SOUTH
♠ 3
♡ A Q
♢ —
♣ —

You are South, declaring a Notrump contract, and the lead is in your hand. You could lead a Spade to the Ace and play a small Heart, planning to finesse the Queen if East follows with his Five-spot. And if East has the King of Hearts, this line will win all three tricks.

But suppose the finesse loses, and West captures your Queen with the King. He will now lead the Two of Diamonds, and his lowly deuce will win a second trick because you and dummy both have to discard! So you wind up with only one trick instead of two.

In view of this potential catastrophe, you should take this finesse *only if you need all three tricks to make your contract*. If two tricks will suffice, *don't* finesse; ensure victory by cashing the two Aces. *Don't risk your contract for an overtrick!*

Another terrible time to finesse is when your side has so many cards in the suit that power play is more likely to produce extra winners:

NORTH (DUMMY)

♡ J 10 7 6 3

SOUTH (DECLARER)

♡ A K 9 4 2

The lead is in dummy, and dummy doesn't have any other entries. The Jack is led, East plays a nondescript Heart, and you are faced with the moment of truth. If you go up with the Ace, the lead will be in your hand and you'll never be able to finesse. But if you finesse the Jack and it loses, you'll feel very silly! Once East follows suit, West can't have more than two Hearts (since there were only three of them missing to begin with); so if West does have the Queen, it must drop under your Ace and King. What should you do?

Barring some sensational clue to the contrary, the right play is to go up with the Ace and then lead the King. This gains whenever West has either the singleton or the doubleton Queen, and loses only when East began with all three of the outstanding Hearts.

To avoid headache misery, here's a fast-acting table that shows when *not* to finesse:

YOUR SIDE'S HONORS	ENEMY HONORS	BARRING STRONG CLUES TO THE CONTRARY, *Don't* FINESSE IF YOUR SIDE HOLDS:
A Q	K	11 or more cards
A K J	Q	9 or more cards
A K Q 10	J	7 or more cards
A K Q J 9	10	Any number of cards

Note that in the preceding example, life is simple if dummy has some entries. Start by cashing the Ace. If West discards, you'll know that you have to enter dummy and finesse against East's Queen; while if West follows suit, your next play will be the King of Hearts.

WINNING TRICKS BY TRUMPING

If your partnership is suffering from a severe shortage of high cards, Trump Power may enable you to rout the enemy:

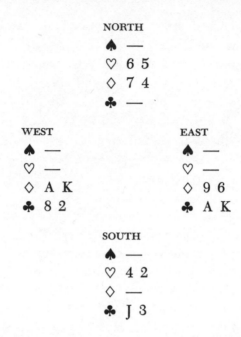

You (South) are the declarer, and the lead is in your
hand. If the contract is Notrump, you can lead Hearts and
win the first two tricks; but you must then surrender the
rest of the tricks to the opponents' power winners. But if
your side has been clever enough to make Hearts the
trump suit, correct play will win all four tricks! Lead a
Club, and ruin East's visions of glory by ruffing with the
Five of Hearts. The lead is now in dummy, so play a Diamond and make West very unhappy by trumping with
the Two of Hearts. Now lead your remaining Club and
trump it in dummy, and then ruff dummy's last Diamond.
Be careful, however, *not* to lead any Hearts. If you do,
you'll run out of them too soon, and the opponents will
escape the ruffing menace and capture a trick or two
with their honors.

DRAWING TRUMPS

The defenders are also permitted to make thorough nuisances of themselves by ruffing, and this dastardly practice should be prevented whenever possible:

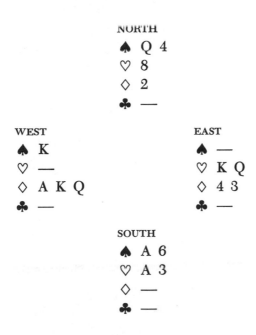

NORTH
- ♠ Q 4
- ♡ 8
- ◊ 2
- ♣ —

WEST
- ♠ K
- ♡ —
- ◊ A K Q
- ♣ —

EAST
- ♠ —
- ♡ K Q
- ◊ 4 3
- ♣ —

SOUTH
- ♠ A 6
- ♡ A 3
- ◊ —
- ♣ —

You are declaring a Spade contract from the South chair, and you need all four tricks to make it. The lead is in your hand. How do you proceed?

This position is fraught with traps and pitfalls! If you cash the Ace of Spades, play a Spade to the Queen (which is now high), and then lead a Heart to the Ace, East will win the last trick with the King of Hearts and wreck your contract. And if you start off by leading the Ace of Hearts, West will happily destroy you by trumping it with the King of Spades!

The winning strategy is to first eliminate the enemy ruffing power (**draw trumps**), and then make good use of your own. Begin by cashing the Ace of Spades. Now that the opponents are trumpless, cash the Ace of Hearts and trump your low Heart in dummy.

Although extracting the enemy trumps is highly desirable, eliminating *dummy's* trumps may be a major disaster:

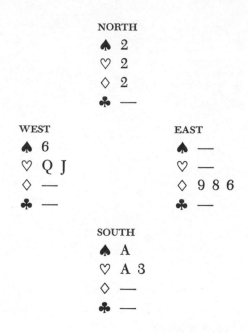

NORTH
♠ 2
♡ 2
◇ 2
♣ —

WEST
♠ 6
♡ Q J
◇ —
♣ —

EAST
♠ —
♡ —
◇ 9 8 6
♣ —

SOUTH
♠ A
♡ A 3
◇ —
♣ —

You (South) are once again declaring a Spade contract, you have the lead, and you urgently require all three tricks. Now you cannot afford to draw trumps, for dummy's supply will perish along with West's and you'll lose the last trick to the Queen of Hearts. Therefore, your only chance is to cash the Heart Ace and ruff your Three of

Hearts in dummy, hoping that neither of these tricks falls victim to an enemy ruff.

TAKING A DISCARD

Careful preparation will sometimes be necessary in order to use your trumps to best advantage:

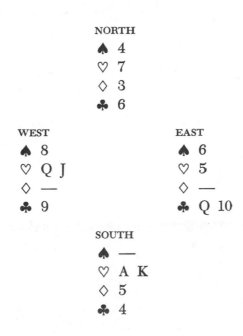

NORTH
♠ 4
♡ 7
♢ 3
♣ 6

WEST
♠ 8
♡ Q J
♢ —
♣ 9

EAST
♠ 6
♡ 5
♢ —
♣ Q 10

SOUTH
♠ —
♡ A K
♢ 5
♣ 4

You are South, Diamonds are trumps, and you need all four tricks to make your contract. The lead is in your hand. What is your plan?

You have three sure winners in the red suits, but you must do something about the Club loser that is leering at you. The right plan is to cash the Heart Ace and then lead the King of Hearts, *discarding a Club from dummy*.

The King is a sure winner, so there is absolutely no reason to trump it; and this inspired maneuver voids dummy of Clubs without losing any tricks in the process. Now you can lead your Four of Clubs and ruff it with the Three of Diamonds, and your own trump easily takes the last trick.

Taking a discard from your own hand can also be very effective:

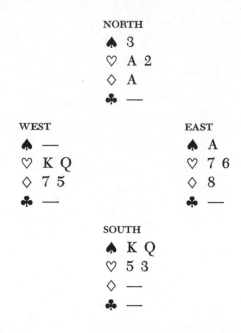

NORTH
♠ 3
♡ A 2
◇ A
♣ —

WEST
♠ —
♡ K Q
◇ 7 5
♣ —

EAST
♠ A
♡ 7 6
◇ 8
♣ —

SOUTH
♠ K Q
♡ 5 3
◇ —
♣ —

Spades are trumps, and West leads the King of Hearts. How do you direct operations from the South seat in order to win three tricks?

Since the opponents have the unbeatable Ace of Trumps, you must win the first trick with the Heart Ace in order to

have any chance. If you now lead a Spade, East will win
with the Ace and return a Heart; and since both you and
dummy must follow suit, you can't prevent West from
winning with his Queen. Therefore, quickly cash dummy's
Ace of Diamonds and discard your remaining Heart. Now
you don't care if the opponents gain the lead and play
Hearts, for you are able to ruff.

THE RUFFING FINESSE

Trump Power may create an unusual kind of finesse:

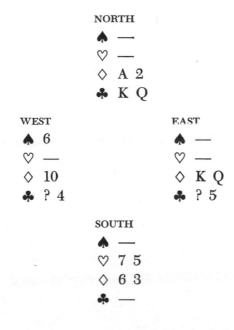

NORTH
♠ —
♡ —
◇ A 2
♣ K Q

WEST
♠ 6
♡ —
◇ 10
♣ ? 4

EAST
♠ —
♡ —
◇ K Q
♣ ? 5

SOUTH
♠ —
♡ 7 5
◇ 6 3
♣ —

Hearts are trumps, and North (dummy) has the lead.
You (South) can see three certain winners, but one
opponent is making life difficult by clinging to the Ace of

Clubs. Is there any way to win four tricks?

Since your trumps outrank the Club Ace, you can actually finesse against it by leading a Club honor from dummy. If East plays the Ace, trump it; then lead a Diamond to the Ace and discard your losing Diamond on dummy's promoted Club honor. If instead East plays his Five-spot, discard a Diamond and hope that West cannot produce the Club Ace. *Don't* cash the Diamond Ace first, for you'll need it as an entry to the good Club if East decides to cover the first Club lead.

LENGTH WINNERS

Even meek and unassuming small cards can turn into powerful winners if they are contained in a long suit:

NORTH
♠ —
♡ —
◇ 8 6 5
♣ 4 2

WEST
♠ —
♡ —
◇ 10 7 4
♣ A K

EAST
♠ 7
♡ —
◇ J 9
♣ 7 5

SOUTH
♠ —
♡ —
◇ A K Q 3 2
♣ —

You are South, declaring a Notrump contract, and you have the lead. You win the first three tricks by leading out your Diamond honors, whereupon your low cards take the last two tricks because everyone is out of Diamonds.

Note that you will fare much worse if East's Nine of Diamonds is exchanged with West's King of Clubs, giving West 10 9 7 4 of Diamonds and the Club Ace. Now West is able to follow suit to the fourth round of Diamonds, his Ten wins the trick, and he takes the last trick as well with his Ace of Clubs. This implies that your ability to turn low cards into length winners often depends on how the enemy cards in that suit are divided. It also implies that you should *count* the number of cards that have been played in important suits, so that you'll know whether or not your small cards are length winners!

UNBLOCKING

At times, careful attention to the size of your spot cards will be necessary in order to cash all your length winners:

NORTH (DUMMY)

◇ K Q 6 4 3 2

SOUTH (YOU)

◇ A 9 8 5

Since the opponents have only three cards in Diamonds, they cannot prevent you from running the entire suit; but you may stop yourself if you're not careful! Suppose you cash the Ace of Diamonds, lead the Five-spot to dummy's King, and then cash the Queen. When you next play Diamonds, your own Nine-spot will be high and will win the trick, *and the lead will be in your hand.* Unless dummy happens to have an entry in a different suit, therefore, the remaining two good Diamonds will be hopelessly stranded.

One excellent way to prevent this disaster is to get rid of your medium-sized Diamonds as soon as possible. After cashing the Diamond Ace, lead the *Nine-spot* to dummy's King. Then lead the Queen and play your *Eight* of Diamonds.* Now you can lead dummy's Six-spot and underplay with your Five, keeping the lead in dummy so you can cash the other two Diamonds.

CREATING ENTRIES

During some deals, you will desperately need extra entries to dummy; while on other occasions, you'll urgently require additional entries to your hand. Some long suits can serve either purpose if handled correctly:

NORTH (DUMMY)

♣ K 6 4 3

SOUTH (YOU)

♣ A Q 7 5

If you need a second entry to dummy, cash the Ace and Queen and then lead the *Seven-spot* to dummy's King. If the enemy Clubs divided 3–2, dummy's Six-spot will now be an entry. But if you need a third entry to your

---

* If the enemy Diamonds divide 2–1, you can instead win the third round in your hand with the Eight-spot and then overtake your Five with dummy's Six.

hand, play the *Five-spot* to dummy's King and hope that the suit splits 3–2, so that your Seven will be an entry on the fourth round of Clubs.

HAND EVALUATION: PREDICTING YOUR TRICK-TAKING ABILITY DURING THE AUCTION

Success at bridge requires good bidding as well as skillful play. If you bid for more tricks than you can make, you'll have to pay a penalty; while if you languish in a part-score (or game) when you are cold for game (or slam), you'll blow a sizable profit. To avoid these sad fates, you must *accurately evaluate your trick-taking potential during the auction;* and each of the possible sources of tricks—high cards, ruffing, and length winners—must be given careful consideration.

HIGH-CARD POINTS (HCP)

Higher cards are more likely to win tricks during the play than are lower ones. A good way to evaluate this aspect of your strength is by assigning a certain number of *points* to each high honor that you hold:

$$
\begin{aligned}
\text{Ace} &= 4 \text{ points} \\
\text{King} &= 3 \text{ points} \\
\text{Queen} &= 2 \text{ points} \\
\text{Jack} &= 1 \text{ point}
\end{aligned}
$$

These points have nothing at all to do with the scoring; they are merely a way of *predicting your ability to take*

tricks. The *sum* of your **High-Card Points** (**HCP**) reveals
the total high-card power of your hand:

	(a)	♠ K 6 4 3	(b)	♠ A Q 6 2
		♡ Q 9 7		♡ K 10 7
		◇ A 8 2		◇ A 8 3
		♣ J 10 5		♣ K 9 5

Hand (a) is worth 10 HCP: 4 for the Ace, 3 for the
King, 2 for the Queen, and 1 for the Jack. Hand (b), however, is worth 16 HCP (8 for the two Aces, 6 for the two
Kings, and 2 for the Queen). Thus, hand (b) rates to
take more tricks than hand (a)—and should therefore be
bid more strongly.

Although the HCP method is simple and effective, it is
far from infallible. At times, adjustments will be necessary
in order to avoid overestimating or underestimating your
trick-taking ability:

1. Add a point if you have a lot of Tens and Nines. Tens
and Nines aren't powerful enough to be awarded any
HCP, but having a great many of them is likely to mean
an extra trick or two during the play.

**2. Add a point or two if most of your HCP are in
Aces and Kings, and subtract a point or two if most of
your HCP are in Queens and Jacks.** Watch out for hands
like these:

(a) ♠ Q J 6 3   (b) ♠ A K 6 3
     ♡ Q J 9   ♡ A K 7
     ◇ A J 8   ◇ A 9 3 2
     ♣ Q J 7   ♣ 10 8

Hand (a) appears to be worth 14 HCP, but the unusual abundance of Queens and Jacks makes this total misleading. These lower honors are actually worth a fraction *less* than the 2 and 1 HCP accorded to them, so this hand is worth only about 12 or 13 HCP. Conversely, Aces and Kings are worth a bit *more* than the 4 and 3 HCP allotted to them; so the HCP for hand (b) add up to about 19 points.

3. Add a point for a King or Queen in a suit bid by your partner. A King or Queen is likely to be of particular value if it meshes well with partner's length and strength:

(a) PARTNER   (b) PARTNER
    ♠ A Q 6 3 2   ♠ A Q 6 3 2
    ♡ 3   ♡ 3

    YOU   YOU
    ♠ 7 5 4   ♠ K 5 4
    ♡ K 4 2   ♡ 6 4 2

In example (a), you're going to have to scratch and scramble for tricks. If Spades are trumps, your King of Hearts could easily be wasted on a trick that partner captures by ruffing; or it could fall victim to the enemy Ace. In case (b), however, you can readily take five tricks if Spades split 3–2 because your well–located King solidifies partner's holding. Of course, it's thoroughly illegal to look at your partner's hand during the auction; but he'll often send up a flare by bidding his long and strong suits. Therefore, a King or Queen in a suit bid by your partner is worth an extra point. (The Ace is already fully valued and needs no further increase.)

4. Deduct one point for each unprotected lower honor. If your lower honors aren't accompanied by enough other cards in the same suit, they could easily be captured by the opponents. Therefore, deduct one point for each of the following that you hold:

SINGLETON	DOUBLETON
K	A J
Q	K Q
J	K J
	Q J, Q 10,
	or Q x*
	J 10 or J x

Even these adjustments won't turn the HCP method into an exact science; but when close decisions must be made, they'll help you choose between aggressiveness and conservatism.

---

* In bridge literature, the symbol "x" stands for *any spot card* (Nine through deuce).

DISTRIBUTION POINTS (DP)

When you have counted your High-Card Points, you must then consider your ruffing potential. A *short side suit* is particularly valuable for ruffing purposes, for you'll soon run out of cards in that suit and be able to play a trump; and having *more trumps* will enable you to ruff more often and take more tricks. To evaluate both of these factors, assign **Distribution Points (DP)** to your short suits in the following way:

SITUATION	DISTRIBUTION POINTS
You are the opening bidder, or *you* have the long suit, or you have *3-card support* for *partner's* long suit	Void = 3 points Singleton = 2 points Doubleton = 1 point
Partner has (and bids) the long suit and you have *4-card or longer support* for it (and plan to play there)	Void = 5 points Singleton = 3 points Doubleton = 1 point
Partner has (and bids) the long suit and you have *0–2 card support* for it, and/or playing in Notrump is likely	*All* DP = 0

When you have superb support for a suit bid by your partner (and plan to play in that denomination), your ruffing power is increased; and this is reflected by an increased amount of Distribution Points for your short suits.* However, don't count any Distribution Points if you are likely to wind up in Notrump, or if partner owns the long suit and you have terrible support. Short suits are only useful for ruffing purposes, and you can't trump anything if you don't have any trumps!

Let's look at some examples:

(a)	♠ A K J 3 2	(b)	♠ Q 8 7 4
	♡ K 7 6 4 3		♡ 5
	♢ 2		♢ A 7 6 4 3
	♣ 7 6		♣ 10 9 5

Under normal conditions (as when you are the opening bidder), hand (a) is worth 14 points: 11 HCP, 2 DP for the singleton Diamond, and 1 DP for the doubleton Club. Hand (b), however, is worth only 8 points (6 HCP and 2 DP for the singleton Heart).

Now let's suppose that partner opens the bidding with One Spade when you hold hand (b). Your singleton Heart increases in value to 3 DP because of the extra ruffing power provided by your fine Spade support, so your hand is now worth 9 points. If, however, partner misguidedly elects to open with One Heart, don't count any DP at all! A good trump suit is still to be found and your ruffing power is as yet nonexistent, so your hand is worth

---

* Increased DP are counted only by the *supporting* hand because ruffs in that hand are made with trumps that would otherwise fall uselessly under ones led by partner, and therefore produce extra tricks. Ruffs in the long trump hand, however, aren't as likely to yield additional tricks because those trumps probably would have been length winners anyway.

only 6 points. Finally, if partner opens with One Club, your support for his suit is neither very good nor very bad. Count the normal 2 DP for your singleton, showing that your hand is worth 8 points in support of Clubs.

LENGTH POINTS (LP)

Long suits are a third potential source of tricks. However, predicting your ability to develop length winners is a rather complicated affair! It depends on both the length *and strength of* the suit, and it is also partly indexed by your Distribution Points (since you can't be very long in one suit unless you are quite short somewhere else). Therefore, some bridge authorities ignore **Length Points (LP)** entirely. Rather than go to this extreme, however, a rough (and fairly simple) approximation can be used with good effect:

SITUATION	LENGTH POINTS
Solid suit (headed by K Q J 10 or better); or a *strong* suit (headed by K J 10 or better) *for which partner has shown good support*	1 point for the 5th card, and 2 points for every card thereafter
Strong suit (headed by K J 10 or better) which has *not* been supported by partner	1 point for the 6th card and every card thereafter

Weak long suits are more difficult to evaluate. Your best course will often be to avoid counting any Length Points at all for sketchy suits; but if partner's bidding promises fine support, adding some Length Points may be justified. Thus, this aspect of hand evaluation must remain ambiguous until you are more experienced and can apply your own judgment. Finally, if your hand is wildly distributional, abandon the point count entirely and count tricks instead; the point count method is least accurate with freak hands.

Here are some examples:

(a)　♠ A K 9 6 3 2　　(b)　♠ A K Q J 4 3 2
　　　♡ A 5　　　　　　　　♡ A J 10 6 5
　　　◇ 10 3 2　　　　　　◇ A
　　　♣ 9 4　　　　　　　　♣ —

Hand (a) is worth 14 points: 11 HCP, 1 DP for each doubleton, and 1 LP for the sixth Spade. If partner makes a bid that shows good Spade support, revise your LP to 3 (1 for the fifth Spade and 2 for the sixth Spade); your hand is now worth 16 points. This increase reflects your improved prospects for building length winners in Spades.

The potential of a freak hand like (b) is better evaluated in terms of tricks than in points; with any sort of luck in the Heart suit, you should have at least ten winners. In unusual cases like this, the total point count of 29 (19 HCP, 5 DP, and 5 LP for the solid Spade suit) is of secondary importance—and probably rather inaccurate as well.

IMPORTANT POINT-COUNT TOTALS

Every deal contains a total of 40 HCP. A hand of average strength contains 10 HCP, 1 or 2 DP, and 0 or 1 LP, or about 12 total points. The exact number of points needed to make game or slam depends on the specific situation, but the following guidelines will be accurate in many instances:

COMBINED PARTNERSHIP TOTAL	PROBABLE RESULT
25 points or less	Part-score
26 points	Game in Notrump, Spades, or Hearts
29 points	Game in Diamonds or Clubs
33 points	Small slam
37 points	Grand slam

Minor-suit contracts require more tricks for game and hence more points, so you'll often aim for Notrump even when your side has a good Club or Diamond fit. On occasion, bad luck will wreck a sound game contract; while a game bid on meager values may survive because of good luck (or bad defense!). Usually, however, game should be bid when your partnership has 26 points or more and avoided when your combined assets add up to 25 points or less.

BIDDING AS A LANGUAGE: THE ART OF COMMUNICATING WITH YOUR PARTNER

To arrive at the right contract, you must consider partner's assets as well as your own. You usually won't have enough winners in your own hand to make game or slam, so you'll have to find out if partner has the extra help that you need; and you also must discover the best denomination in which to play. Therefore, your partnership must use the bidding to *exchange information about your respective strengths and distributions.*

Only the legal bidding language may be used to describe a hand, so it's vital to understand what the various bids mean. For example, a well-conducted auction might proceed as follows (with the opponents passing throughout):

PLAYER	BID	UNSPOKEN MESSAGE TO PARTNER
You	One Spade	"I've got an above-average hand with a decent Spade suit. If you can provide some help, we might be able to make game."
Partner	Two Spades	"I have good Spade support and some strength, but my hand is very mediocre. I don't think we can make game unless your hand is very powerful."
You	Four Spades	"It is! But don't bid any more; we don't have any chance for slam."
Partner	Pass	"OK!"

Thus, a good game contract is reached even though neither partner has enough strength to risk bidding Four Spades on his own. When two people talk in different languages, however, very bad things are likely to happen:

CHARLES: "Bonjour, monsieur. Comment allez-vous?"*
BILL: "Three pounds of sugar."

Obviously, this conversation is in serious trouble! And the same type of disaster happens in bridge:

PLAYER	BID	UNSPOKEN MESSAGE TO PARTNER
Partner	One Heart	"I've got an above-average hand with a pretty good Heart suit."
You	Three Hearts	"Great! I've got fine Heart support and enough strength to guarantee game. I'm not bidding Four Hearts only because I want to leave some bidding room to explore for *slam*. So whatever you do, *don't* pass!"
Partner	Pass	"I have no extra strength beyond what I've already promised, so I can't bid any more."
You	$#(!*$!!	(censored)

* French for "Good day, sir. How are you?"

Here, a cold game is missed because the two partners have quite different ideas about the meaning of the Three Heart bid. Actually, both interpretations are reasonable ones. There is no one best method for assigning meanings to bids (**bidding system**), and even experts disagree as to the best "language" to use. In order to prevent catastrophes like this one, therefore, you and your partner must know and understand the meanings of the various bids that may arise *before* you sit down to play.

So that you can play bridge without suffering through pre-game bidding discussions that last for hours (or weeks), this book will emphasize standard bidding methods that are used by the majority of bridge players. In same cases, however, new and more effective alternatives will be recommended—with the proviso that you discuss them with your partner *in advance,* so as to ensure that both of you are speaking the same language.

OPENER'S STRATEGY

To make the opening bid (first call other than a pass), you need a hand that is clearly above average in trick-taking potential. Normally, this means a hand worth *at least 14 total points.* The point-count method is not an exact science, however, so feel free to open a 13-point hand that has unusually good features. Also, the requirements for opening may be relaxed by a point or two when partner has passed originally (is a **passed hand**).

BALANCED HANDS

In addition to your strength, the distribution of your

hand has a strong effect on your bidding strategy. Suppose you hold one of the following hand patterns:

1. 4-3-3-3 (that is, four cards in one suit and three cards in every other suit).
2. 4-4-3-2.
3. 5-3-3-2, where the five-card suit is a *minor*.

These **balanced** hands have a mere 0 or 1 DP, so they are unlikely to produce many ruffing winners. In addition, your partnership is less likely to have a good trump suit— one where your side outnumbers the opponents by at least 8 cards to 5—because you don't have a long suit of your own to contribute. (The five-card suit in Pattern 3 isn't terribly exciting because it is a minor, and game in a minor requires a huge number of tricks). An eventual suit contract isn't out of the question, since a 4-4 *major*-suit fit is usually a superior resting place (and since *partner's* hand may be very unbalanced). Aside from this important possibility, however, you should suggest a Notrump contract to your partner when your hand is balanced.

One simple (but terrible!) way to do this would be to open any balanced hand with One Notrump. This highly misguided approach would drive your partner crazy; he'd have no idea as to your strength, and your auction would soon degenerate into blind guesswork. Instead, keep him well informed (and your side on the way to the right contract) by using one of the methods summarized in Table 1.

TABLE 1. TWO METHODS FOR OPENING A BALANCED HAND

Method 1. "Standard"—used by most average bridge players

STRENGTH	STRATEGY
From a "good" 13 total points up to 15 HCP	Open with one of a suit. Plan to proceed conservatively at your next turn to bid.
16 to 18 HCP	Open with One Notrump.
19 to 21 HCP	Open with one of a suit. Plan to proceed aggressively at your next turn to bid.
22 to 24 HCP	Open with Two Notrump.
25 to 27 HCP	Open with Three Notrump.

Method 2. "Modern"—superior to Standard, but requires prior discussion and agreement with your partner

STRENGTH	STRATEGY
From a "good" 13 total points up to 15 HCP	Same as Standard.
16 to 18 HCP	Same as Standard.
19 to 20 HCP	Open with one of a suit. Plan to proceed aggressively at your next turn to bid.
21 to 22 HCP	Open with Two Notrump.
23 to 24 HCP	Open with Two Clubs. Plan to bid Two Notrump at your next turn.
25 to 27 HCP	Open with Two Clubs. Plan to make a single jump to Three Notrump at your next turn.

The superior "modern" method is favored by the majority of today's bridge experts, but is not yet common among average players. Hopefully, you'll be able to find a partner who is willing to learn and use it. But since this won't always be possible, it's also desirable to learn the "standard" method so that you'll be able to play with any partner.

The modern approach to opening balanced hands makes good use of a clever device: The **artificial** (or **conventional**) Two Club opening bid. There is no bridge law that a Club bid must show a good Club suit, or that a Notrump bid must express a desire to play in Notrump; it is entirely legitimate for a bid to convey information that has nothing at all to do with the denomination named in that bid.* The artificial Two Club opening sends the following message: "Partner, I've got a super hand, but I may have nothing at all in Clubs. *Don't pass!* If you're broke, bid Two Diamonds, and I'll tell you more about my hand at my next turn." This procedure does away with the awkward Three Notrump opening, which crowds your own bidding to a very painful degree. It also enables you to define your strength more precisely in many instances. And, as we will see in the following section, the artificial Two Club opening is also superior to standard methods when you have a very powerful *un*balanced hand.

---

* Weird artificial bids designed solely to annoy the opponents, however, are out of bounds. Also note that you are required to inform the opponents, before the bridge game begins, about any artificial bids that you and your partner are using; and that artificial bids must be made in the same way as natural ones (special wording or tones of voice are strictly illegal).

TABLE 2. TWO METHODS FOR OPENING AN UNBALANCED HAND

Method 1. "Standard"—used by most average bridge players

STRENGTH	STRATEGY
Very long and strong suit (Q J 10 x x x x or better); very weak in other suits (*not* strong enough for a one-bid)	Open with *three or four* of your long suit. Bid for about three tricks more than you can make in your own hand if you are *not* vulnerable; overbid by about two tricks if you are vulnerable.
From a "good" 13 to 24 total points, including at least 10 HCP	Open with *one* of a suit. Plan to define your strength and distribution more precisely at your next turn.
25 or more total points, or a powerful freak hand worth at least 9 tricks	Open with *two* of a suit.

Method 2. "Modern"—superior to Standard, but requires prior discussion and agreement with your partner

One-bids:	Same as Standard.
Two-bids:	Open Two Clubs with any hand worth 25 or more total points. Plan to bid your real long suit at your next turn.
Three-bids:	Same as Standard.
Four-bids:	Same as Standard.

UNBALANCED HANDS

The "standard" and "modern" procedures for opening an **unbalanced** hand (one with *2 or more DP*) are summarized in Table 2. Opening bids of one of a suit, which are the same in both methods, cover a very wide range of strengths and distributions. For your one-bid, you might have a 13-point minimum or a booming 24-point power-house; and you might have a nearly balanced pattern such as 4–4–4–1 or 5–4–2–2, or a wild freak like 7–4–2–0 or 8–5–0–0. Therefore, it's especially important to define your strength and distribution more accurately at your next turn to bid, as we will see in the next chapter.

Opening bids of three or four of a suit use up so many levels of bidding that intelligent cooperation with your partner is very difficult. Therefore, both the standard and modern methods use these **preemptive** opening bids only when: (1) you have a suit so long and strong that partner's cooperation in selecting the best denomination isn't necessary, *and* (2) the rest of your hand is so weak that the opponents probably own the balance of power, so you are willing to blockade your own auction (and risk a modest penalty for going down) in order to disrupt their bidding.

The "standard" opening bid of two of any suit shows a hand where you can virtually make game all by yourself. It orders partner *not* to pass, while leaving room below the game level to explore for the best contract (or for slam). Although simple, this approach has serious weaknesses. It wastes four bids—Two Clubs, Two Diamonds, Two Hearts, and Two Spades—on situations that occur very rarely. (The more a hand is above or below average in strength, the less likely it is to occur.) Also, it may well make the subsequent bidding awkward. Therefore, the "modern" method uses the artificial Two Club opening to show *any* hand worth a strong two-bid. After partner's forced response, you show your real suit (and let him know that your hand is unbalanced) by bidding it.*

CHOOSING THE SUIT

When you decide to make a suit opening bid, here's how to choose the right suit:

1. If your longest suit is five or more cards, bid it! In case of ties, bid the *higher-ranking* suit first.

2. If your longest suit is four cards, bid your *longer minor*. If your minor suits are equal in length, bid One Club unless your Diamonds are very much stronger (such as A J x in Diamonds and x x x in Clubs).

Using this procedure, opening bids of One Heart and One Spade promise at least five cards in the bid suit. "Standard" players do open four-card major suits, and this approach is not unreasonable; but **five-card majors**

---

* In addition to making the subsequent bidding easier, the "modern" approach allows opening bids of Two Diamonds, Two Hearts, and Two Spades to be used as *preempts*. These "weak two-bids" show a hand similar to an opening three-bid (strong suit, weak hand) but worth one trick less; and since they arise much more often than strong two-bids, they provide valuable extra opportunities to harass the enemy. A discussion of weak two-bids is beyond the scope of an introductory text, however, and you should wait until you are more experienced before you try them.

are at least as effective,* and are much easier for the new bridge player to learn. If your partner knows or is willing to learn five-card majors, agree in advance to use them. If he refuses, or if you don't get an opportunity to discuss this issue, continue to use your five-card major strategy when *you* open the bidding. In this one instance, nothing very terrible will happen to your side if your bidding languages are slightly different; and methods for responding to four-card major openings will be discussed later on, so you'll be able to bid accurately after your partner's opening bids.

ILLUSTRATIVE EXAMPLES

Let's take a look at some examples of opener's strategy in action. In each case, you are the dealer (and hence the first to speak); test yourself by deciding on your call before reading the answer that follows.

(a)	♠ K Q 7 6	(b)	♠ 7 3	(c)	♠ A Q 6 2
	♡ A 6 4 3		♡ Q J 5 2		♡ 10 8 7
	◇ 10 5 2		◇ Q J 4		◇ A 9 3
	♣ Q 8		♣ K Q J 6		♣ K 9 5

With hand (a), you should pass. You have only 11 points (11 HCP and 1 DP, less one point for the doubleton Queen), and you need at least a good 13-count to open.

Also pass with hand (b). Deduct a point or two when most of your HCP are in Queens and Jacks; this hand is really worth only about 11 points.

---

* They do make it somewhat harder to find a valuable 4–4 major-suit fit, but discovering a useful 5–3 fit becomes much easier.

Hand (c), however, should be opened with One Club. Although it is worth only 13 points, and although the 4–3–3–3 shape is the weakest one of all (no DP or long suits), there are several important redeeming features. You have half the Aces in the deck, and a King; and your well-located Queen could easily become a finesse winner because you have the Ace in the same suit. Your good holding in Spades, the highest-ranking (and hence most important) suit, is another valuable asset. Therefore, the scales tip in favor of opening. Your longest suit is four cards, so check for your longer minor; and since your minors are equal in length and not greatly different in strength, prefer the cheaper one. Plan to proceed conservatively at your next turn, showing a balanced hand too weak to open with One Notrump.

(d) ♠ A J 6 3   (e) ♠ A 10 6 2   (f) ♠ K 7
     ♡ 7 2   ♡ A Q 8 5   ♡ K J 9 5
     ◇ A J 5 2   ◇ Q 7 3   ◇ A J 10 7
     ♣ K 10 9   ♣ K 6   ♣ K Q 4

Hand (d) should be opened because it is worth 14 points (13 HCP and 1 DP). Since your longest suit is four cards, bid One Diamond (your longer minor).

Hand (e) should also be opend with One Diamond, since you're not quite strong enough for a One Notrump opening bid (only 15 HCP). When you open in a suit, *do* count your DP; your hand is currently worth 16 total points. But if it becomes apparent that you're going to wind up in Notrump, forget your DP and reduce the total value of your hand to 15 points. You can't ruff anything in a Notrump contract, so a short suit is no longer an asset.

Hand (f) is balanced and has 17 HCP, so it meets all the requirements for the highly descriptive One Notrump opening. Since you are bidding Notrump, *don't* count any DP for the doubleton Spade. But if a good suit fit (such as a 4–4 Heart fit) later appears on the horizon, add the DP and increase the value of your hand to 18 points; your short suit will have some value in a contract where you can ruff the third round of Spades.

(g) ♠ K J 10   (h) ♠ K Q 4 2   (i) ♠ J 10 6 2
     ♡ Q 9 8   ♡ K 3   ♡ A K 7 4
     ◇ A 7 5 4 2   ◇ A Q 9 8 3   ◇ A
     ♣ A Q   ♣ K 9   ♣ A 8 6 3

Hand (g) has 16 HCP and balanced distribution and the five-card suit is a *minor*, so open with One Notrump. Remember that game in Notrump requires *two* tricks less than game in a minor!*

Hand (h) has 17 HCP, but is too unbalanced for a Notrump opening bid. Start off with One Diamond, and evaluate your hand at 19 total points.

Hand (i) is also too unbalanced to open in Notrump, so bid One Club. Your hand is worth 18 points (16 HCP and 2 DP).

---

* The decision is much tougher if your five-card suit is a *major*. The recommended procedure is to open with one of your major if it is fairly strong, but to bid One Notrump if it is quite weak (say, J x x x x or worse).

(j) ♠ A K 6 3   (k) ♠ K Q J 6   (l) ♠ A Q 8
    ♡ A K 7   ♡ A J 10 4   ♡ K Q 3
    ◇ A 9 3 2   ◇ A Q 6   ◇ A K Q 7
    ♣ 10 8   ♣ A Q   ♣ A Q 10

As we observed some pages back, hand (j) is actually worth about 19 HCP because all of the honors are Aces and Kings. Therefore it is too strong for a One Notrump opening bid, so start with One Diamond and plan to proceed very aggressively at your next turn.

Hand (k) is substantially stronger than hand (j), and must therefore be bid differently. Using standard methods, show your 23 HCP and balanced distribution by opening with Two Notrump. If you and your partner have agreed upon the modern approach, however, start with Two Clubs (artificial *and forcing*) and plan to rebid Two Notrump over partner's probable Two Diamond response.

Hand (l) is so powerful that drastic methods are required! "Standard" players must open with Three Notrump to show 26 HCP and a balanced hand, which is likely to crowd their bidding to an alarming degree. "Modern" players open with Two Clubs, planning to make a single jump to Three Notrump at their next turn to bid.

        (m) ♠ A 9 8 7 6   (n) ♠ 7
            ♡ K 4 2   ♡ A 10 9 8 7
            ◇ Q 9 3   ◇ A Q 10 9 7
            ♣ 10 5   ♣ 10 8

            (o) ♠ K J 10 4 3 2
                ♡ A J 9
                ◇ Q 8 7
                ♣ 6

You would bid Spades if you were going to open hand (m), but opening would be a serious error! Your hand is worth only 10 points (9 HCP, 1 DP), so you have no choice but to pass.

Hand (n), however, is worth a One Heart opening bid. You have 10 HCP and 3 DP, and having all your high cards in long suits and numerous Tens is worth an extra point. With two five-card (or two six-card) suits, break the tie by bidding the *higher-ranking* suit first.

Hand (o) should be opened with One Spade. You have 14 points: 11 HCP, 2 DP, and 1 LP for the sixth card in the strong Spade suit.

(p) ♠ K
     ♡ J 8 7 6 3
     ◇ A K 9 5
     ♣ A Q 10

(q) ♠ A K J 7 6
     ♡ A Q 8 3
     ◇ K 10
     ♣ A 2

(r) ♠ A
     ♡ A K Q 10 9 4
     ◇ K Q J 9 6
     ♣ 2

Bid One Heart with hand (p). Although your suit is weak, *any* five-card (or longer) suit may be bid at the one-level. Your hand is worth 18 points (17 HCP and 2 DP, less one point for the singleton King of Spades).

Although hand (q) is very powerful, you should still open with One Spade. You are not strong enough to bid two of a suit (23 points), and your good five-card *major* and unbalanced distribution rule out a Notrump bid. *

Hand (r), however, is well worth a strong two-bid. You have 10 or 11 probable tricks in your own hand (5 or 6 in Hearts, 4 likely winners in Diamonds, and the Ace of Spades), and your point total is an awesome 26-count (19 HCP, 4 DP, and 3 LP for the fifth and sixth cards in the solid Heart suit). Using standard methods, open with Two Hearts; while if you have adopted the modern approach, start with Two Clubs and bid Hearts at your next turn. These openings order partner not to pass, and leave room below the level of game to seek out the best contract.

(s) ♠ K Q J 9 8 7 5 3   (t) ♠ K Q 10 9 8 6 3
    ♡ 7 3 2   ♡ K 3
    ◇ Q   ◇ K 6
    ♣ 6   ♣ 7 3

(u) ♠ 8
    ♡ J 9 7 6 4 3 2
    ◇ A 8
    ♣ Q 10 5

Hand (s) is a typical *preemptive* opening bid. Your enormous suit gives you every right to insist upon playing in Spades regardless of partner's holding, and your weak side values strongly suggest that the opponents are hoping

---

* If you find this procedure somewhat unsettling, you're entirely right! The wide range of strength covered by one-bids is a significant weakness of normal bidding methods, and is one important reason why some bidding theorists have sought to develop better systems.

to do some bidding of their own. Foil them by opening with Four Spades if you are *not* vulnerable, overbidding by *three* tricks more than you can take in your own hand. If instead you *are* vulnerable, the penalties for going down are greater; so overbid by just *two* tricks and open with Three Spades. (Since preemptive-type hands are freaks, it is easier—and more accurate—to count tricks instead of points.) And once you have opened with a preempt, *don't* succumb to the temptation to bid again! Partner knows everything about your hand and you don't know a thing about his, so let him call the signals for the rest of the auction.

Although the Spade suit in hand (t) is excellent, you should open with One Spade. Your strength in the other suits indicates that your team could easily own the balance of power, and the opponents may be hoping for nothing more than to get on to the next deal in a hurry. Therefore, a preempt is all too likely just to foul up your own auction. (16 points)

Hand (u) has a weak suit and good side values, which is exactly the opposite of a sound preempt. Therefore, your best course of action is to pass. (10 points)

BRIDGE MOVIE 2: LOOK BEFORE YOU LEAP

You (South) deal yourself the following hand:

♠ K 7 3
♡ A K 8 2
◇ 10 9
♣ A Q 6 5

What call do you make?

ANSWER: With 16 HCP and a balanced hand, your correct call is One Notrump.

West passes, North raises to Three Notrump, and East passes. You have reached a game contract and partner's bid announces that there is no chance for slam, so you pass; and West also passes, ending the auction.

West leads the Five of Spades, and partner puts down the following dummy:

NORTH
♠ A 10
♡ 7 6 3
♢ K Q J 3 2
♣ 8 4 3

Opening
Lead: ♠ 5

SOUTH
♠ K 7 3
♡ A K 8 2
♢ 10 9
♣ A Q 6 5

Now that dummy has turned up with the Ace of the suit led by West, should you quickly play it and clinch the first trick for your side?

ANSWER: Absolutely not! As the title of this Bridge Movie suggests, declarer should always take a few moments to consider his overall battle plan before playing any cards at all.

You need *nine* tricks to make your Three Notrump contract, and you have only five sure power winners (two in Spades, two in Hearts, and the Club Ace). The Diamonds are likely to provide the four additional tricks that you need, so long as you can *lead* them enough times. Your own hand, however, is rather short in Diamonds; so you'd better save the Ace of Spades for use as an entry to dummy later on.

You play dummy's Ten of Spades, and East tops it with the Queen. *What do you play from your hand?*

ANSWER: The King of Spades. If you play low and allow East's Queen to win, he'll undoubtedly lead another Spade and drive out dummy's Ace—exactly what you wish to avoid.

NORTH
♠ A
♡ 7 6 3
◇ K Q J 3 2
♣ 8 4 3

What do you lead to the second trick, and what card do you play from dummy?

SOUTH
♠ 7 3
♡ A K 8 2
◇ 10 9
♣ A Q 6 5

ANSWER: Lead the Ten (or Nine) of Diamonds, and play dummy's deuce.

When you don't have enough power winners to make your contract, you must build up the additional tricks that you need before your protection in weaker suits is driven out. Therefore, attack Diamonds immediately. Your Ten is equivalent in value to dummy's honors and you have another Diamond to play if you hold the trick, so overtaking would be a serious blunder.

West plays the Five of Diamonds on your Ten and East contributes the Six of Diamonds, producing the following situation:

NORTH

♠ A
♡ 7 6 3
♢ K Q J 3
♣ 8 4 3

SOUTH

♠ 7 3
♡ A K 8 2
♢ 9
♣ A Q 6 5

What do you lead to the next trick, and what card do you play from dummy?

ANSWER: Lead the Nine of Diamonds. If West plays low, *overtake* with one of dummy's honors!

Once again, you must look ahead carefully in order to avoid leaping to a faulty conclusion. Your fiendish opponents are trying to foil your plans by withholding their Ace of Diamonds, and they may do so again on this trick. If so, playing dummy's Three of Diamonds will be ruinous! The lead will remain in your hand, and you won't have any more Diamonds. If you try to recoup by entering dummy with the Spade Ace and leading a Diamond, the defenders will take their Ace and cash a gruesome number of Spade tricks; and even when you do regain the lead, the good Diamonds will be hopelessly stranded in an entryless dummy.

West plays the Four of Diamonds on your Nine-spot, so you overtake with dummy's Jack, and East plays the Seven of Diamonds. The position now is:

NORTH

♠ A
♡ 7 6 3
◇ K Q 3
♣ 8 4 3

What is your next play?

SOUTH

♠ 7 3
♡ A K 8 2
◇ —
♣ A Q 6 5

ANSWER: The King (or Queen) of Diamonds. Thanks to your foresight on the preceding trick, the lead is in dummy and you can continue to establish the Diamonds.

East tops dummy's King with the Diamond Ace, you discard the Five of Clubs, and West pitches the Seven of Clubs. The remaining cards are:

NORTH
♠ A
♡ 7 6 3
♢ Q 3
♣ 8 4 3

East now leads the Eight of Spades, you play your Three-spot, West contributes the deuce of Spades, and dummy's Ace wins.

Lead: ♠ 8

SOUTH
♠ 7 3
♡ A K 8 2
♢ —
♣ A Q 6

What are your plans for the next two tricks?

ANSWER: First cash dummy's Queen of Diamonds and then lead the Three of Diamonds, discarding two small cards from your hand.

By *counting* the all-important Diamond suit, you can tell that there is exactly one Diamond left in the hands of the enemy. Your side began with seven cards in Diamonds, so the opponents started with six of them. Both East and West followed suit to the first two rounds of Diamonds, using up four of their supply, and East produced one more Diamond on the third round of the suit. Thus, five of the six missing Diamonds have been played; and the remaining one must fall under your Queen, making the Three-spot a length winner. But you must cash your Diamonds now, since you can see that dummy will never again have the lead.

You do so, discarding your two low Hearts; East plays the Eight of Diamonds, on the Queen and discards the Four of Hearts on dummy's Three-spot, while West discards the Nine of Clubs and the Nine of Hearts. The position now is:

NORTH

♠ —
♡ 7 6 3
◊ —
♣ 8 4 3

Since the lead is in dummy, you might as well take the Club finesse. Right?

SOUTH

♠ 7
♡ A K
◊ —
♣ A Q 6

ANSWER: Wrong! Lead to one of your Aces and quickly cash your other two power winners. (Then surrender.)

You have won six tricks thus far and three more winners are in plain sight, so your contract is assured. But if you take the Club finesse and it loses, West may be able to cash enough length winners in Spades to defeat you! And this is just what would happen, for the complete deal is:

NORTH
♠ A 10
♡ 7 6 3
◇ K Q J 3 2
♣ 8 4 3

WEST
♠ J 9 6 5 2
♡ J 9
◇ 5 4
♣ K J 9 7

EAST
♠ Q 8 4
♡ Q 10 5 4
◇ A 8 7 6
♣ 10 2

SOUTH
♠ K 7 3
♡ A K 8 2
◇ 10 9
♣ A Q 6 5

The bidding:

SOUTH	WEST	NORTH	EAST
1 NT	Pass	3 NT	Pass
Pass	Pass		

The moral: *Don't risk your contract for an overtrick!*
(And *look* before you leap!)

The Auction Continues

At each turn to bid, your strategy depends on how much you know about your partner's hand. When he makes a bid that gives precise information about his strength and distribution (a **limited** bid), you should take charge of the auction. First, determine your side's chances for game (or slam) by *adding your points to those he has promised.* Then proceed as follows:

YOUR SIDE'S TOTAL	YOUR STRATEGY
Cannot equal at least 26 points	*Stop* in the first playable contract you can find.
Might equal 26 points	*Invite* partner to go on to game.
Must equal at least 26 points	*Insist* on reaching game.

Often, however, partner will have to leave you pretty much in the dark by making a relatively ambiguous (**un-**

limited) bid. When this happens, light a candle by *making the most descriptive bid that you can.* You don't have enough data to decide about game or slam, so share information until one of you can correctly make a limited bid. Then, the other partner will be able to take charge and guide the auction to a good resting place.

RESPONDER'S STRATEGY

RESPONDING TO ONE NOTRUMP

Raises. Suppose that partner opens the bidding with One Notrump, a *limited* bid that shows precisely 16–18 HCP and balanced distribution. What call do you make with each of these hands?

(a) ♠ 7 4	(b) ♠ 8 7 6	(c) ♠ K 6 2
♡ K J 6	♡ 9 2	♡ 5 4
◊ 8 7 5 3	◊ A J 10 4	◊ A J 9 8
♣ Q 10 6 4	♣ K 10 9 3	♣ K 10 7 3

Your own distribution is also balanced and there is no chance of finding a valuable 4–4 major-suit fit, so Notrump should be a fine spot in each case. The only remaining question is how much to bid, and you should pass with hand (a). Your 6 HCP bring your side's total to only 22–24 points, so the 26 points needed to bid game are out of reach.

With hand (b), game is an "iffy" proposition. You have 8 HCP, so you belong in game if partner has 18 points (or a "good" 17-count). But if he has only 16 points (or a "bad" 17-count), you should stop in a partial. The solution is to **invite** game by raising to Two Notrump, which asks partner to go on to Three Notrump with a maximum but to pass with a minimum.

Hand (c) is worth 11 HCP, so your side has between 27 and 29 points. Jump directly to Three Notrump, a **sign-off** that orders partner to pass regardless of his holding.

When *slam* appears on the horizon, the Three Notrump signoff must be rejected:

(d) ♠ K Q 8   (e) ♠ K Q 3   (f) ♠ A K 9
      ♡ A J 9   ♡ A Q 8   ♡ A J 5
      ◇ K Q 10 6   ◇ A 10 9 7   ◇ K Q 10
      ♣ J 10 7   ♣ Q J 10   ♣ A Q 10 7

Game should certainly be reached with hand (d), since you have an impressive 16 HCP. If partner has 17 or 18 points, however, your side will own the 33 points needed to bid a small slam. Therefore you should raise to Four Notrump, which asks partner to bid Six Notrump with a maximum but to pass with a minimum.

With hand (e), however, you should bid Six Notrump yourself. You have 18 HCP, so your side must total at least 34 points. And with hand (f), proceed all the way to Seven Notrump! Your hand is worth 23 HCP and partner has at least 16, so the most that the opponents can own is one lonely Jack.

Major-suit jumps. The following hands require a different strategy:

(a) ♠ A K J 7 6   (b) ♠ 9 8
    ♡ 3 2   ♡ K Q 10 8 6 3
    ◇ 7 4 3   ◇ K 8 6
    ♣ K J 8   ♣ 5 3

If partner opens with One Notrump and you hold hand (a), you are clearly strong enough to insist on reaching game. Unfortunately, you can't tell whether to bid it in Notrump or Spades! You need partner's help in selecting the best spot, and you can get it by *jumping* to Three Spades. This bid promises five or more Spades and is **forcing to game**; partner is under orders to continue bidding until game is reached. If he has three-card or longer Spade support, an eight-card (or longer) fit is assured and he will raise to Four Spades.* With only a doubleton Spade, however, he will return to Three Notrump.

With hand (b), however, your side belongs in Hearts even if partner has only two-card support. (He can't have less, since his One Notrump opening promises balanced distribution.) And you belong in game, since your hand is worth 11 points (8 HCP, 1 LP, and 2 DP now that a good suit fit has been found). Therefore, jump directly to Four Hearts (a *signoff*).

Minor-suit jumps. Since game in Clubs or Diamonds requires eleven tricks, hands with long *minor* suits are often best played in Notrump:

---

* As was noted in the preceding chapter, the normal minimum for a good trump suit is one where your side outnumbers the opponents by at least 8 cards to 5.

(a) ♠ K 8 7   (b) ♠ A 7
     ♡ K 10 3   ♡ K J 3
     ◇ K 10 9 7 6   ◇ 10 3
     ♣ 4 2   ♣ Q J 9 6 4 2

With either of these hands, your best course is to raise partner's One Notrump opening to Three Notrump. Bidding only Two Notrump with hand (a) would put too much pressure on partner, who might pass with 17 points; and bidding your long suit in either example would make life unnecessarily difficult for both of you, since the nine-trick Notrump game is very likely to be the best contract. Therefore, the game-forcing responses of Three Clubs and Three Diamonds are used only with a very unbalanced hand, and responses of *four* of a minor are not even used as natural bids.

Two-level responses: The Stayman Convention. Even experts have been known to create incredible disasters by forgetting their own bidding conventions (and during important tournaments!), so it's understandable if you are somewhat leery of artificial bids. One convention is so valuable, however, that it must be considered mandatory for all good bridge players. It is called the **Stayman Convention**, and is used to locate one of those important 4–4 major-suit fits. Here's how it works:

When partner opens with One Notrump, a Two Club response is *artificial and forcing* and says nothing at all about your holding in Clubs. It conveys three messages to your partner:

1. Your hand is *at least strong enough to invite*

game (you have *at least 8 HCP*).

2. You have at least one four-card (or longer) *major* suit.

3. You want him to bid a four-card (or longer) *major* suit if he has one.

If partner doesn't happen to have a four-card major, he lets you know by bidding Two Diamonds (also an *artificial* bid). After hearing his reply, you may invite game by raising his major to the three-level or by returning to Two Notrump; but if you are strong enough to insist on game, you must now bid it directly.*

To illustrate, suppose that partner opens with One Notrump and you hold any of these hands:

(a) ♠ A 9 6 3   (b) ♠ A Q 10 6   (c) ♠ 8
    ♡ 4 2   ♡ K J 9 5   ♡ 9 7 6 5
    ◇ K 4 3   ◇ 8 3   ◇ Q 4 3 2
    ♣ J 10 9 6   ♣ 10 7 4   ♣ K J 5 3

Hand (a) is just strong enough to invite game, so you can seek out a 4–4 Spade fit by bidding Two Clubs. If partner bids Two Spades, raise to Three Spades; while if he bids Two Diamonds or Two Hearts, return to Two No-

---

* Or make a forcing bid, such as a jump in a new suit. Incidentally, there is no general agreement as to what the One Notrump bidder does with *two* four-card majors; an acceptable (if arbitrary) procedure is to bid Spades first. If the Stayman bidder returns to Notrump, opener then goes ahead and shows his Hearts.

trump. In either case, he will pass with a minimum but go on to game with a maximum.

With hand (b), however, you must make sure that game is reached. Start off by bidding Two Clubs. If partner bids two of a major, raise directly to *four;* while if he bids Two Diamonds, jump to *Three* Notrump. Both actions are signoffs, informing partner that he is expected to pass.

A Stayman response with hand (c) might score an occasional triumph by locating a good Heart fit, but is more likely to get you into serious trouble. You cannot risk getting to game in Notrump when you have only 6 HCP, so the right action is to pass.

Here's a typical example of the benefits of the Stayman Convention:

OPENER	RESPONDER
♠ A Q 6 3	♠ K J 7 5
♡ 6 3 2	♡ J 4
♢ K Q J	♢ 10 8 3
♣ K Q 2	♣ A J 10 9

OPENER	RESPONDER
1 NT	2 ♣
2 ♠	4 ♠
Pass	

A Three Notrump contract would be in serious danger because of the Heart situation. Thanks to Stayman, however, the excellent Spade game is reached with little difficulty. Nor is this the only advantage:

(a) ♠ Q 9 7 6 4   (b) ♠ A 9 7 4 3
    ♡ 2   ♡ K 10 3
    ◇ J 6 3   ◇ J 10 8
    ♣ 8 5 4 2   ♣ 7 6

(c) ♠ K Q 6 4 2
    ♡ A Q 7 5
    ◇ 10 8
    ♣ 10 2

Game is clearly out of reach with hand (a). However, a Spade partial is likely to be much superior to Notrump even if partner has only two-card support, for you'll surely be able to score several tricks by ruffing. If you play in Notrump, your weak long suit could easily be entirely wasted; and if it doesn't produce any tricks, your side will be in grave difficulty! In situations like this, you reap another important (albeit indirect) gain from using Stayman: *Responses of Two Spades, Two Hearts, and Two Diamonds are signoffs,* showing at least a five-card suit and a weak hand.* Therefore, you can promptly and easily reach the best contract by bidding Two Spades. Players who don't use Stayman must pass, since all of their two-level responses are invitational to game.

With hand (b), you would like to invite game and mention your respectable Spade suit. You can't respond Two Spades, since that would be a signoff, so begin with a Two Club response. If partner bids Two Diamonds or Two

---

* Exception: Opener may raise to three with excellent support for responder's suit and a super maximum, especially if he can now count a DP and push his total up to 19.

Hearts, now bid Two Spades. Your continued interest in the suit promises at least a five-carder, and your original Stayman response ensures that you are worth a game invitation. If partner happens to bid Two Spades over your Two Club response, you may raise to game.

Also respond Two Clubs with hand (c). If partner bids two of a major, raise to four. If he bids Two Diamonds, however, make sure that game is reached (and offer him a choice of game contracts) by *jumping* to Three Spades (forcing to game).

RESPONDING TO HIGHER-LEVEL NOTRUMP OPENINGS

An opening bid of Two or Three Notrump, or an artificial Two Club opening followed by a rebid of Two or Three Notrump, also *limits* opener's hand very precisely. Here again, you should add your points to partner's and evaluate your chances for game or slam. If game is out of reach, you must pass; *all* responses to higher-level Notrump openings are forcing to game. Otherwise, the responses are similar to those following a One Notrump opening bid.

To illustrate, let's suppose that partner opens with a "standard" 22–24 point Two Notrump. What call do you make with these hands?

(a)	♠ 7 4	(b)	♠ J 8 6	(c)	♠ Q 9 7 4
	♡ 9 6 5 3 2		♡ Q 6 3		♡ K 10 6 2
	◇ 4 3 2		◇ Q 10 7 5		◇ 7 3 2
	♣ J 10 3		♣ 6 4 2		♣ 10 8

Hand (a) is so ghastly that game is out of reach despite partner's powerhouse. Therefore you must pass.

With hand (b), however, you should raise to Three Notrump. Your 5 HCP may not seem like much, but they bring your side's total to 27–29 points.

You should also insist on reaching game with hand (c), but first check out a possible 4–4 major-suit fit by bidding Three Clubs (*Stayman*). If partner bids three of a major, raise to four; while if he denies a four-card major by bidding Three Diamonds, return to Three Notrump.

	(d)	♠ K 8 3	(e)	♠ A J 8 6 3
		♡ Q 7 6		♡ 10 7
		◊ Q 10 7 3		◊ J 6 3
		♣ K 6 2		♣ 6 4 2

Hand (d) is worth 10 HCP, so you belong in a small slam if partner has 23 or 24 points. Invite him to bid it by raising to Four Notrump.

Hand (e) is worth a game bid, but either Notrump or Spades could be the right spot. Therefore, bid Three Spades (which is forcing to game) and let partner make the final decision. He will raise to Four Spades with three-card or longer support, but will bid Three Notrump if he has only a doubleton Spade.

RESPONDING TO ONE OF A SUIT

Suppose that partner opens with One Diamond and you have:

♠ 9 8
♡ K Q 10 8 6 3
♢ K 8 6
♣ 5 3

When you held this hand several pages back and partner opened with *One Notrump,* you reached the right contract in a single bid by jumping to Four Hearts. After the *One Diamond* opening, however, you've got more work to do! If partner happens to have a 13-point minimum and a void in Hearts, you probably don't belong either in game or in Hearts; while if he has a 23-point powerhouse and four or five cards in Hearts, a Heart *slam* should be a fine spot. Thus, you can't possibly determine the right contract at this point—or even make a sensible decision about your chances for game.

The culprit responsible for this confusion is the *unlimited* opening bid of One Diamond. It shows anywhere from 13 to 24 points, and partner's distribution could be wildly unbalanced or perfectly balanced (but too weak for a Notrump opening bid). With so little information to go on, even a world champion couldn't take charge of the auction; so the best strategy after an *un*limited bid is to *share information* by making the *most descriptive* bid that you can.

The pass. If you have only 0 to 5 points, you should describe this tragic state of affairs by *passing.* You might conceivably miss a game if partner has a rockcrusher, but bidding is too likely to get your side overboard. However, don't hesitate to respond if you can somehow finagle your count up to 6 points:

(a) ♠ 10 6 4   (b) ♠ A J 9 6 5
♡ J 7 6 3 2   ♡ 10 8 3
♢ J 7 3   ♢ 10 9 2
♣ 3 2   ♣ 3 2

If partner opens with One Club, you should pass with hand (a). You have only 2 points (no DP, since you have only two-card support for partner's suit), so you aren't even close to a response.

With hand (b), however, you should bid One Spade.

TABLE 3. TWO METHODS FOR RAISING PARTNER'S
OPENING BID OF ONE OF A MAJOR SUIT

Method 1. "Standard" raises—used by most average bridge players

RESPONSE	STRENGTH	SUPPORT
Raise to Two (*limited; not forcing*)	7–10 points	At least 3 cards. (Those using "four-card majors" need 4-card support.)
Raise to Three (*limited; forcing to game*)	13–15 points	At least 3 cards. (Those using "four-card majors" need 4-card support.)
Raise to Four (*semi-preemptive*)	12–15 points, but less than 10 HCP	At least 5 cards, plus 5–5–2–1 or even more unbalanced distribution.

You have 5 HCP, and your respectable five-card Spade suit is an excellent "plus" feature.

Priority 1: Raise partner's major. When you are strong enough to respond, the most descriptive bid you can make is to raise partner's *major* suit. The requirements for this top priority response are summarized in Table 3.

Let's suppose that partner opens with One Heart and you are using "standard" raises. Bid Two Hearts with either of these hands:

Method 2. "Modern" raises—superior to Standard, but require prior discussion and agreement with your partner

RESPONSE	STRENGTH	SUPPORT
Raise to Two (*limited; not* forcing)	6–9 points	Same as Standard raise to two.
Raise to Three (*limited; not* forcing)	10–12 points	Same as Standard raise to three.
Three Notrump (*artificial; forcing*)	13–15 points*	Same as Standard raise to three.
Raise to Four (*semi- preemptive*)	Same as Standard raise to four.	

* *Do* count your Distribution Points, since you are really raising opener's suit and have no intention of ending up in Notrump.

(a) ♠ 6 2   (b) ♠ 10
    ♡ Q 10 6   ♡ 9 8 6 3
    ◇ K 10 7 5   ◇ Q 10 7 3 2
    ♣ 10 9 8 4   ♣ A 5 4

Hand (a) just qualifies for the single raise, since it is worth 7 points (5 HCP, 1 DP, and one extra point for the Queen in partner's suit). The singleton in hand (b) is worth 3 DP because you have four-card support for partner's suit, so the 6 HCP bring the total to 9 points.

(c) ♠ K 7   (d) ♠ 10 2
    ♡ A 8 7 6   ♡ A 10 8 7 3
    ◇ K J 6 5 3   ◇ K J 10 6 5
    ♣ 10 9   ♣ 6

Hand (c) is a typical "standard" raise to Three Hearts. Hearts is clearly an ideal spot and the double raise describes your hand perfectly (13 points, good support), so there is no reason to mention the Diamonds.

Hand (d) qualifies for a jump to Four Hearts. You should have a good play for your contract, and your preemptive tactics will make it hard for the opponents to locate a good contract of their own. (12 points)

Although the standard approach is widely used, it runs into trouble with hands like these:

(e) ♠ 7 3   (f) ♠ K J 8
    ♡ A 9 4 2   ♡ K 8 6 3
    ◇ J 10 5 3   ◇ A 3 2
    ♣ 8 4 2   ♣ 10 4 3

You *should* be able to raise partner's One Heart opening bid in either of these examples, since your fine Heart support is an extremely important aspect of your hand. But you can't! Hand (a) is worth only 6 points, and is therefore too weak for a single raise.* Hand (b) adds up to 11 points, which makes it too strong for a single raise but too weak for a game-forcing double raise.

The modern method avoids these problems by using the Three Notrump response as *artificial and forcing,* showing a hand like (c). It agrees upon Hearts as the trump suit, and orders partner to continue bidding until at least Four Hearts is reached. This clever device allows you to bid Two Hearts with hand (e) and Three Hearts (*invitational, not* forcing) with hand (f).

Priority 2: Jump to Two Notrump. If you are unable to raise partner's major (perhaps because you don't meet the requirements, possibly because he didn't happen to open with one of a major), the next most descriptive bid you can make is a game-forcing jump to Two Notrump. This *limited* response shows precisely 13–15 HCP, *balanced* distribution, and **stoppers** (*protected* honors) in all unbid suits. If partner opens with One Spade, jump to Two Notrump with:

♠ 5 2
♡ K Q 8
◇ A J 7 3
♣ K J 10 7

* Since the "limited bid strategy" works well only when partner's strength is defined within a very narrow range, increasing the range of the "standard" single raise to 6–10 points would only substitute one evil for another.

If partner opens with one of a minor, however, you may *not* jump to Two Notrump because the unbid Spade suit is not stopped.

Priority 3: Bid a new suit. If you can't raise partner's major or jump to Two Notrump, the next best choice is to bid a new suit:

RESPONSE	MEANING
New suit bid at the *one*-level	6–17 points, 4-card or longer suit. (*Unlimited; forcing**)
New suit bid at the *two*-level without jumping	11–17 points, 4-card or longer suit. In an emergency, a 3-card *minor* may be bid. (*Unlimited; forcing**)
Single *jump* in a new suit	18 or more points, good 5-card or longer suit. (*Forcing to game*)

Choose the *longest* suit that does not violate the strength requirements. If you have two or three eligible *four*-card suits, bid the *cheapest* one first. With two *five*-card or two *six*-card suits, however, start with the *higher-ranking* suit (just as you would when opening the bidding).

Let's look at some examples. In each case, partner's opening bid is shown directly above your cards.

---

* Exception: If you are a *passed hand*, these bids are *not* forcing. Your failure to open indicates that you have at most a "bad" 13-count, so partner may pass if he has opened light in third position.

(a) *One Diamond* (b) *One Diamond*
   ♠ Q 10 8 3   ♠ K J 7 6
   ♡ 5 3 2   ♡ K 10 4 2
   ◊ 8   ◊ 3
   ♣ A 10 9 6 3   ♣ A 10 5 2

(c) *One Club*
   ♠ A 8 6 5 3
   ♡ K Q 10 7 2
   ◊ 5 4
   ♣ 9

Hand (a) is worth 6 points (*no* DP, since your support for opener's suit is terrible!). You need at least 11 points to bid a new suit at the *two*-level, so a Club response must be rejected. Luckily, a *one*-level response requires only 6 points, so you can—and should—bid One Spade.

Bid One Heart with hand (b), choosing your *cheapest four*-card suit. If partner has four-card support, he will raise; if not, he can easily show a four-card Spade suit at the one-level. And if he does neither, you probably don't belong in a major-suit contract (11 points).

With hand (c), however, you should bid One Spade (the *higher-ranking five*-card suit). Partner is not allowed to bid a *three*-card major, so you may have to bid both of your suits in order to locate an eight-card fit; and if you do mention the Hearts at your next turn, partner will be able to return to Spades without increasing the level of bidding. (9 points)

(d) *One Diamond*   (e) *One Spade*
  ♠ K 10 8 5   ♠ 7 5
  ♡ 2   ♡ A K J 10 7 6
  ◇ A 6 3   ◇ K 9
  ♣ K J 10 7 6   ♣ A 5 4

(f) *One Heart*
  ♠ K J 8
  ♡ K 8 6 3
  ◇ A 3 2
  ♣ 10 4 3

Bid Two Clubs with hand (d). You have more than enough strength to bid at the two-level (13 points, including 2 DP for the singleton with three-card support for partner's suit), so start with your longest suit.

Hand (e) is worth a *jump shift* to Three Hearts. You have 18 points: 15 HCP, and 3 LP for the nearly solid Heart suit.

As we have seen, "standard" players can't raise Hearts with hand (f). They dredge up a Two Club or Two Diamond response and then support Hearts as cheaply as possible at their next turn, thereby showing a hand worth a raise to "2½ Hearts."

Priority 4: Raise partner's minor or bid One Notrump. The "last resort" department includes three possibilities:

RESPONSE	MEANING
Raise to two of partner's *minor*	7–10 points, good 4-card or longer support, unbalanced hand. (*Limited; not* forcing)

| Raise to three of partner's *minor* | 13–15 points, very good 4-card or longer support. (*Limited; forcing*) |
| One Notrump | 6-10 points, no other good bid to make. (*Not* forcing) |

For example, suppose that partner opens with One Diamond and you hold any of these hands:

(a) ♠ Q 10 5
♥ J 9 6
♦ 2
♣ A 10 8 7 6 3

(b) ♠ K 8 3
♥ J 10 6
♦ A 10 7 2
♣ 9 7 4

(c) ♠ 9 8 7
♥ 4
♦ A 10 7 2
♣ Q 10 4 3 2

Hand (a) is not strong enough for a Two Club response (only 7 points), so you must bid One Notrump in spite of your unbalanced distribution. A One Notrump response is also the best choice with a balanced hand like (b). With hand (c), however, a raise to Two Diamonds is preferable. And if you have the following hand, Three Diamonds is the only conceivable response:

♠ K 8 6
♥ A 7 4
♦ A J 9 5 3
♣ 10 5

RESPONDING TO A STRONG TWO-BID

"Standard" two-bids. If you are using "standard" methods and partner opens with two of a suit, *don't pass!* You are under strict orders to bid even if you are completely broke, so respond as follows:

RESPONSE	MEANING
Two Notrump	0–6 points, any distribution. *Artificial* "negative" response.
Three Notrump	7–9 HCP, relatively balanced distribution.
Single raise	7 or more points, at least 3-card support.
Double raise	4-card or longer support; *No outside Ace, King, void, or singleton.*
New suit bid without jumping	7 or more points, at least Q J x x x in bid suit.
Single *jump* in a new suit	*Absolutely solid* suit—at least A K Q J x x.

All of these responses are *forcing to game*, with one exception: If you make the negative Two Notrump response and partner rebids his suit at the three-level, you are permitted to pass. However, don't bail out if you have any values at all:

♠ 8 6 5
♡ 7 3
♢ 10 9 4
♣ K 7 6 4 3

Partner opens with Two Spades, and you respond Two Notrump (no choice, since you have less than 7 points). If he now returns to Three Spades, your King and ruffing value in Hearts are enough to justify a raise to Four Spades.

The artificial Two Club opening. If you are using the artificial Two Club opening to show any hand worth a strong two-bid, respond Two Diamonds (*artificial* and "negative") with 0–6 points. A Two Notrump response is *positive*, showing 7–9 HCP and a balanced hand; and the bid of a new suit is also positive, promising at least 7 points and a good five-card or longer suit.

RESPONDING TO A PREEMPT

When partner opens with a preemptive bid, you are in charge of the auction. Since he has promised a superb suit, you should almost always play the hand right there (even if you are void!). To decide how much to bid, simply count *tricks* instead of points.

To illustrate, suppose that partner opens with a non-vulnerable Three Spades and you hold any of these hands:

(a) ♠ 6
♡ A K 6 3
◇ A 10 7 3
♣ A Q 8 2

(b) ♠ 4 3
♡ K J 7 3
◇ K J 8
♣ K Q 7 2

(c) ♠ 3
♡ Q 4 3
◇ 10 8
♣ A J 9 8 6 5 2

Partner has promised six tricks (three less than his non-vulnerable preempt) and hand (a) is worth 4 or 5 tricks, so proceed to Four Spades. A Three Notrump response would be a serious error, as you'll get cut off from partner's long suit if he has no outside entries. His hand:

♠ K Q J 10 8 7 5
♡ 5 2
◇ 9 6 2
♣ 4

Pass with hand (b). You have only about two tricks to add to partner's six and the opponents probably can't make anything, so there is no reason to take any action.

Also pass with hand (c). Partner's suit is better than yours, and fighting with him can only enrich the enemy.

SUBSEQUENT BIDDING

A complete discussion of bidding would take many more pages than you would care to read (or I'd care to write!). Before leaving this important topic, however, let's take a brief look at your strategy during the later stages of the auction.

OPENER'S REBID

Rebids after a Notrump opening. If you have opened with a Notrump bid, remember that partner is in charge of the auction. At your next turn to bid, follow his instructions: Pass a signoff, accept an invitation with a maximum but pass with a minimum, answer partner's Stayman bid by showing a four-card major if you have one, and so on.

Rebids after opening with one of a suit. When you open with one of a suit and partner makes a *limited* response, you're the boss. Suppose you hold:

♠ A 5 2
♡ A Q 10 6 3
◇ 7 6
♣ K 4 3

You open with One Heart, and partner makes a "standard" raise to Two Hearts. His bid promises 7–10 points and you have 15 (13 HCP, 1 DP, and 1 LP for a strong five-card suit that has been supported), so your side's total is 22–25 points. You can see that game is out of reach and you're in an eminently playable contract, so you should pass. If instead partner makes a "standard" raise to Three Hearts, however, you should go on to Four Hearts. He has shown 13–15 points, so your combined assets add up to 28–30 points—enough for game.

When your opening bid of one of a suit is followed by an *unlimited* response, help clarify matters by making the most descriptive bid that you can. If partner bids a new *major* suit and you have four-card or longer support, you should raise his suit: Raise from one to two with 13–16 points, from one to three with 17–19 points, and from one all the way to four with 20 points or more. For example:

(a) ♠ A J 7 4   (b) ♠ A J 3 2
     ♡ Q 5 3   ♡ K Q 9
     ◊ K 10 8 6   ◊ K Q 8 3 2
     ♣ A 2   ♣ 5

        (c) ♠ A K 10 9
             ♡ A K Q
             ◊ K J 8 4
             ♣ 4 2

You open each of these hands with One Diamond and partner responds One Spade, showing at least four cards in Spades and from 6 to 17 points. Raising partner's *major* suit takes priority over a Notrump rebid, so bid Two Spades with hand (a). Hand (b) is worth 18 points (15 HCP plus 3 DP for the singleton with four-card support for partner's suit), so jump to Three Spades. And with hand (c), proceed directly to Four Spades.

If you can't raise partner's major, it's desirable to bid a new four-card or longer *major* suit if you can do so without misleading partner about your strength. (Some common rebids by opener, and the strength and distribution promised by each, are summarized in Table 4 on page 132–3.) Failing this, an appropriate Notrump rebid is likely to be ideal if your hand is relatively balanced; while with an unbalanced hand, you may bid a new (minor) suit, or rebid your first suit if it contains at least *five* cards.

RESPONDER'S REBID

When you face the challenge of responder's second bid, keep these helpful hints in mind:

1. If your previous response was the first limited bid made by your side, partner is in charge of the auction. Follow his instructions.

2. If opener's rebid was the first limited bid made by your side, you're in charge. Use the "limited bid strategy."

3. Be ready to bail out in a hurry if the hands fit badly and game is out of reach, even if the contract is not ideal. Suppose you hold either of these hands:

(a)   ♠ A J 6 3   (b)   ♠ A J 10 7 6 3
        ♡ 7 4 2   ♡ 8 6 5
        ♢ 6   ♢ 6
        ♣ Q 9 6 5 3   ♣ J 10 8

Partner opens with One Diamond, you respond One Spade, and he rebids Two Diamonds. With hand (a), you should *pass*. Your Spades are far too weak to rebid and any other action is at least invitational to game, so quit before it's too late! With hand (b), however, bid Two Spades. Your suit is impressive *and this bid is a signoff*, so you may safely try to improve the contract.

4. A "preference" does not show any extra strength. In the following situation, it would be an error to bail out too soon:

         ♠ A Q 8 6
         ♡ 10 7
         ♢ 6
         ♣ J 6 5 4 3 2

TABLE 4. SOME COMMON REBIDS BY OPENER AND
THEIR MEANINGS

OPENER	RESPONDER	MEANING OF OPENER'S REBID
1. 1 ♣ 2 ♡	1 ♡	13–16 points, 4-card or longer Heart support. *Limited; not forcing.* (The raise to three shows 17–19 points, and the raise to four shows at least 20 points; both are limited and not forcing.)
2. 1 ◇ 1 ♠	1 ♡	13–18 points, 4-card or longer Spade suit. *Unlimited; not* forcing. Opener must *jump* in his suit with 19 or more points (forcing).
3. 1 ◇ 1 NT	1 ♠	13–15 points, relatively balanced hand. Denies 4-card or longer Spade support. *Limited; not* forcing.
4. 1 ♣ 2 NT	1 ◇	19–21 points, balanced hand, stoppers in all unbid suits. *Limited; forcing to game.*
5. 1 ♡ 2 ◇	1 ♠ (or 1 NT, or 2 ♣)	13–18 points, 4-card or longer Diamond suit. *Unlimited; not* forcing. A new *lower*-ranking suit that is bid at the two-level does

not promise any extra strength. Opener must *jump* in his suit with 19 points or more (forcing).

6. 1 ◇   1 ♠
   2 ♡

At least 17 points, good 4-card or longer Heart suit. *Unlimited; forcing.* Here responder must move up to the three-level if he wishes to go back to Diamonds, so opener must have a strong hand.

7. 1 ♡   2 ◇
   3 ♣

At least 17 points, good 4-card or longer Club suit. *Unlimited; forcing to game.* Opener needs a powerful hand to reach the three-level when no good fit has yet been found.

8. 1 ♡   1 ♠
   2 ♡

13–16 points, at least a 5-card Heart suit. *Limited; not* forcing. (After a One Notrump response, the Two Heart rebid promises at least a 6-card Heart suit.)

9. 1 ♡   1 ♠ (or
   3 ♡   1 NT)

17–19 points, good 6-card or longer Heart suit. *Limited; not forcing.*

10. 1 ◇   1 NT
   2 NT

16–18 HCP, relatively balanced hand. *Invitational to Three Notrump.*

Partner opens with One Heart, you respond One Spade, and he rebids Two Diamonds. Partner's first suit is likely to be longer than his second one and your Heart support is not quite as hideous as your Diamond holding, so return to Two Hearts. This does *not* show any more strength than would a pass of Two Diamonds.

5. *If opener's rebid is anything other than One Notrump, a new suit bid by responder is forcing.* If game is in sight but you're still not sure where to play it, one way to shop around is by bidding a new suit. This orders opener *not* to pass at his next turn.

6. *Use your increased knowledge about opener's hand.* If opener makes a rebid that guarantees a *six*-card or longer suit, you now know that you need only two-card support to ensure an eight-card fit—and to raise.

7. *Don't be a "part-score perfectionist."* Only a small number of bids are available, so most of them must be used as game invitations (or forces). When game is out of reach, therefore, you'll often have to settle for a *reasonable* part-score contract because you simply don't have the bidding machinery to locate the *best* one.

SLAM BIDDING

Slam bidding is difficult even for experts, especially when suit contracts are involved. Owning 33 points is often *not* enough to justify bidding a suit slam, for you must also be able to prevent the opponents from wrecking your contract by cashing two fast winners:

OPENER	RESPONDER
♠ A K 9 6 3 2	♠ Q 8 7 4
♡ K 4	♡ A Q J 9 6
◇ K 5	◇ Q 6 3
♣ K Q 2	♣ 8

Opener has 23 points (18 HCP, 2 DP, and 3 LP in Spades when responder raises) and responder owns 15 points (11 HCP, 3 DP, and 1 point extra for the Queen in opener's suit), so the total is an awesome 38 points. Yet even small slam should not be bid, since the opponents can promptly cash two Aces!

To be sure, this is a rather extreme example of duplication of values. No fewer than 8 HCP are completely wasted: the King and Queen of Clubs and the Queen and Jack of Hearts. Nevertheless, there is an easy way to stay out of slam. It is called the **Blackwood Convention**, and here's how it works:

After a trump suit has been firmly agreed upon, a bid of Four Notrump is *artificial* and asks partner *how many Aces* he holds. (A Four Notrump response to a *suit* opening bid is also Blackwood.) He answers as follows:

5 ♣ = 0 or 4 Aces
5 ◇ = 1 Ace
5 ♡ = 2 Aces
5 ♠ = 3 Aces

If the Blackwood bidder discovers that his side owns all

four Aces and wants to try for a grand slam, he may now inquire about Kings by bidding Five Notrump. (Partner answers in a similar way.) In the preceding example, the correct auction is:

OPENER	RESPONDER
1 ♠	3 ♠
4 NT	5 ◇
5 ♠	Pass

Opener knows that slam is very likely, since he has 23 points and responder has promised at least 13. Fortunately for his side, he takes the precaution of checking for Aces. When his partner turns up with only one, he screeches to a halt in Five Spades—and responder must pass, since the Blackwood bidder is in complete charge of the auction.

Unfortunately, Blackwood is so appealing that most players use it far too often. Here's a typical Blackwood tragedy:

OPENER	RESPONDER
♠ A K 9 6 4 3	♠ Q J 5 2
♡ K Q 3	♡ A J 7
◇ 6 2	◇ 9 8 5
♣ A 8	♣ K Q 3

OPENER	RESPONDER
1 ♠	3 ♠
4 NT??	5 ◇
6 ♠	Pass

Opener is worth 21 points at his second turn to bid (16 HCP, 2 DP, and 3 LP), and responder has shown at least 13. This brings the partnership total to at least 34, so opener launches into Blackwood and bids the slam when he finds that his side is missing only one Ace. However, the opponents happily cash the Ace and King of Diamonds!

This disaster cannot be blamed on Mr. Blackwood, for opener should not have used the convention at all. The Diamond situation was clearly fraught with danger, so he desperately needed to know *which* Aces partner had— *not* how many! Here's how the auction should have gone:

OPENER	RESPONDER
1 ♠	3 ♠
4 ♣	4 ♡
5 ♡	5 ♠
Pass	

Since Spades is clearly established as the trump suit, the Club and Heart bids are slam tries that show **controls** (Aces and Kings). These **cue-bids** reveal that neither partner can do anything about the Diamond problem, and so they stop just in time. Thus, one mark of a good bridge player is that he knows when *not* to use Blackwood!

BRIDGE MOVIE 3: TRUMP POWER

Your partner, North, deals you the following hand:

♠ 5 4
♡ K Q J 9 7
◇ A 5 4 2
♣ 6 5

He starts things off on a promising note by opening with One Club, and East passes. *What call do you make?*

ANSWER: One Heart. Partner's unlimited bid shows anywhere from 13 to 24 points, and from three to eight or nine Clubs. Therefore, your best strategy at this turn is simply to share information. You can't make a major-suit raise (priority #1) or jump to Two Notrump (priority #2), but you do have a good new suit to brag about (priority #3)—and more than the 6 points needed to bid it at the one-level.

West passes, North raises to Two Hearts, and East passes. *Now what call do you make?*

ANSWER: Four Hearts. Partner has just defined his hand within fairly narrow limits, so it's time to take charge of the auction. He has promised fine Heart support and precisely 13 to 16 points, and your hand is worth 13 points for Heart purposes (10 HCP, 2 DP, and 1 LP). This brings your side's total to 26–29 points, so make sure that game is reached (and turn thumbs down on slam) by bidding it directly.

Everyone else passes, ending the auction. West leads the King of Clubs, and you eagerly scan the dummy:

NORTH

♠ A K Q
♡ 5 4 3 2
◇ J 6 3
♣ A 10 2

Opening
Lead: ♣ K

How do you like your contract?

SOUTH

♠ 5 4
♡ K Q J 9 7
◇ A 5 4 2
♣ 6 5

ANSWER: It's a good one! You have five power winners in the side suits and four probable Heart tricks, and you're likely to get the tenth winner that you need by ruffing the fourth Diamond in dummy. However, there is a serious problem: Your potential losers include the Ace of Hearts, two Diamond tricks, and one Club trick, and that's one more than you can afford.

Therefore, what emergency action must you take?

ANSWER: Win the first trick with the Ace of Clubs and

cash dummy's three top Spades, discarding your losing Club on the third round.

The three red-suit losers appear to be unavoidable, so you've got to get rid of that troublesome Club. And there's no time to waste! If you start off by playing trumps, the opponents will win with the Ace and quickly cash a Club trick. You must take the discard immediately, and then use your Trump Power to frustrate the enemy.

You do so, and the opponents gloomily follow suit to each trick with nondescript small cards. The position now is:

NORTH

♠ —
♡ 5 4 3 2
◇ J 6 3
♣ 10 2

SOUTH

♠ —
♡ K Q J 9 7
◇ A 5 4 2
♣ —

How do you proceed from here?

ANSWER: Lead a small Heart from dummy, and put up one of your honors if East plays low. Now that there is no urgent danger, start extracting the enemy trumps so that *they* can't use ruffing power to frustrate *you*.

You lead dummy's Two of Hearts, East plays the Eight

of Hearts, you choose the King, and West wins with the Ace. He returns the Queen of Clubs, with East playing the Club Seven when his turn arrives:

NORTH

♠ —
♡ 5 4 3
◇ J 6 3
♣ 10 2

Lead: ♣ Q   (♣ 7)   *What do you play to this trick and the next one?*

SOUTH

♠ —
♡ Q J 9 7
◇ A 5 4 2
♣ —

ANSWER: Ruff with the Seven of Hearts, and then lead the Queen (or Jack) of Hearts.

In a Notrump contract, you'd be helpless to stop the opponents from winning a ghastly number of Club tricks. But thanks to your invaluable trumps (and your previous Club discard!), you won't suffer a single Club loser— and can promptly get on with the business of drawing trumps.

West plays the Six of Hearts on your Queen, dummy follows with the Three of Hearts, and East discards the Ten of Spades. The current position is:

NORTH

♠ —
♡ 5 4
◇ J 6 3
♣ 10

SOUTH

♠ —
♡ J 9
◇ A 5 4 2
♣ —

Should you play another round of trumps?

ANSWER: Yes. Your side started with nine cards in Hearts and the opponents have played three of them so far, so they've still got one trump left; and you can afford to get it out of the way before it does any damage.

You lead the Jack of Hearts, West follows with the Heart Ten, dummy contributes the Four of Hearts, and East discards the Jack of Spades. The remaining cards are:

NORTH

♠ —
♡ 5
◇ J 6 3
♣ 10

SOUTH

♠ —
♡ 9
◇ A 5 4 2
♣ —

How about yet another round of trumps?

ANSWER: That's a horrible idea! Your count shows that the opponents don't have any more trumps, and you desperately need dummy's remaining Heart for ruffing purposes of your own. Instead, cash the Ace of Diamonds and play another Diamond. As it happens, West wins the second Diamond with the Queen and leads the Jack of Clubs in this position:

NORTH

♠ —
♡ 5
♢ J
♣ 10

Lead: ♣ J *Is your contract assured at this point?*

SOUTH

♠ —
♡ 9
♢ 5 4
♣ —

ANSWER: Yes, so long as you are careful to ruff West's high Club with your Nine of Hearts. When you now lead a Diamond, East tops dummy's Jack with the King and fires back the Nine of Diamonds, whereupon dummy's trump come to the rescue and captures the last trick. Here's the complete deal:

NORTH
♠ A K Q
♡ 5 4 3 2
♦ J 6 3
♣ A 10 2

WEST
♠ 9 8 6
♡ A 10 6
♦ Q 10
♣ K Q J 9 3

EAST
♠ J 10 7 3 2
♡ 8
♦ K 9 8 7
♣ 8 7 4

SOUTH
♠ 5 4
♡ K Q J 9 7
♦ A 5 4 2
♣ 6 5

The bidding:

SOUTH	WEST	NORTH	EAST
—	—	1 ♣	Pass
1 ♡	Pass	2 ♡	Pass
4 ♡	Pass	Pass	Pass

Note that it would be an error to postpone drawing trumps for too long. If you play Diamonds before extracting West's Hearts, he can ruff the fourth round with a trump that will top anything dummy can offer—and that will spell the difference between victory and defeat.

4

Declarer's Techniques

Bringing home a challenging contract is a great deal of fun, and is also eminently profitable. In this chapter, we'll look at as many techniques of declarer play as space permits.

NOTRUMP PLAY

WINNING THE RACE

Time is of the essence in Notrump contracts. The opponents know that you can't ruff anything, so they try to strike at your weak spots and build up enough length winners to defeat you. In order to foil this dastardly plot, you must race to build the number of tricks that you need:

WEST (DECLARER)   EAST (DUMMY)
♠ A 3   ♠ 7 4
♡ K J 5   ♡ A Q 2
◇ 6 5 3   ◇ A Q J 10 2
♣ K Q J 10 9   ♣ 7 4 3

WEST   EAST
1 ♣   1 ◇
1 NT   3 NT
Pass

Let's suppose first that the opening lead is a Heart. This is hardly a terrifying development, since you have *three* Heart stoppers, but the opponents may not continue to be so obliging. If you win the first trick in your hand and try the Diamond finesse, and it loses, they may switch to Spades and drive out your lone stopper in that suit. You'll have only eight winners (four in Diamonds, three in Hearts, and the Ace of Spades); and when you now turn to the Clubs, they'll grab their Ace and run a vast number of Spade tricks. You'll suffer the ignominy of discarding your winners on their good Spades, and your contract will go down the drain.

A far better plan is to *count your tricks* before playing any cards. You have five power winners, and the Clubs must provide the four additional tricks that you need to make your contract. Therefore, win the first trick in whichever hand you please and play Clubs until the opponents take their Ace. If they now switch to Spades, you must quickly cash all of your winners; but if they persist with their futile attack on the Heart suit, you can safely try for some overtricks by taking the Diamond finesse.

Now let's suppose that the opponents start off by leading Spades and driving out your Ace. Since they have established their long suit, losing the lead even once will be fatal! Therefore, the Club plan must be rejected. Luckily, there is an alternative route to nine tricks: One in Spades, three in Hearts, and five in Diamonds if the finesse is successful. The right procedure is to lead a Diamond at once and take the finesse. If it wins, reenter your hand by leading a small Heart to the Jack and repeat it. To be sure, you'll go down an extra trick if the finesse happens to lose, but this is a small price to pay for a chance to make your contract. The opponents are about to win the race, so desperate measures (in the form of trying for nine *fast* winners!) are entirely justified.

EXTRACTING THE STING

When the opponents do strike your weakest link, you can sometimes defuse the threat by breaking their communications:

NORTH
♠ K Q 7
♡ 8 5
◇ A Q 9 8 2
♣ 10 9 7

SOUTH
♠ A 5
♡ A 9 2
◇ J 10 6
♣ A Q J 8 6

SOUTH	NORTH
1 NT	3 NT
Pass	

The hold-up. West leads the Six of Hearts, and East produces the King. Play your deuce and allow the opponents to win the first trick! East continues the assault by leading the Ten of Hearts, and you again **hold up** by playing the Nine-spot. West overtakes with the Jack and plays the Queen of Hearts, you discard dummy's Seven of Clubs, East discards the Two of Clubs, and you must now take your Ace.

Avoiding the danger hand. You've got six power winners, and can easily build three more in either minor suit even if the finesse loses. The problem is that if the opponents gain the lead, they may cash enough Heart tricks to wreck your contract.

Here's where your previous hold-ups pay rich dividends. East has told you that he's now out of Hearts—not in words, of course, but by his discard on the third trick. Only

West can defeat you; he is the **danger hand**, and you must prevent him from gaining the lead. Losing the lead to East, however, will not be fatal. Therefore, lead the Jack of Diamonds and take the finesse if West plays low. As it happens, East wins with the King, but your contract is perfectly safe. He tries vainly to reach his partner's hand by leading a Club, but you go right up with your Ace and cash all of your winners to bring home your game contract. The complete deal is as follows:

NORTH
♠ K Q 7
♡ 8 5
◇ A Q 9 8 2
♣ 10 9 7

WEST
♠ 10 6 3
♡ Q J 7 6 4 3
◇ 7 4
♣ K 3

EAST
♠ J 9 8 4 2
♡ K 10
◇ K 5 3
♣ 5 4 2

SOUTH
♠ A 5
♡ A 9 2
◇ J 10 6
♣ A Q J 8 6

Even if East follows suit to the third round of Hearts, the Diamond finesse is the correct play. West has probably led from a long suit in an attempt to develop some length winners. If Hearts are divided 5–3, East will be out of them at this point (and unable to hurt you). And if East does turn up with another Heart, the suit has divided 4–4—so the opponents can collect only three Heart tricks and one Diamond trick.

Other applications. Hold-up plays are useful in a variety of circumstances, but there are times when they should be rejected. Consider these examples:

NORTH
♡ 4 2

WEST
♡ K Q 10 9 5

EAST
♡ 8 7 6

SOUTH
♡ A J 3

Suppose that Hearts is clearly your weak spot, and West leads the King. Here, a hold-up is an excellent idea. If West continues the suit, he presents you with two stoppers (and two tricks); while if he shifts, you gain valuable time. Winning with the Ace would turn *East* into a danger hand, since you'd be in terrible trouble if he then led through your J 3.

NORTH
♠ 10 2

WEST
♠ Q 9 8 5 4

EAST
♠ K 7 6

SOUTH
♠ A J 3

If West leads the Five of Spades, you should play

dummy's deuce and top East's King with your Ace. The Jack and Ten will now serve as a second stopper, whereas holding up the Ace limits you to one trick.

NORTH

◇ 5 2

WEST

◇ Q 10 7 6 4

EAST

◇ J 9 3

SOUTH

◇ A K 8

West leads the Six of Diamonds, and East puts up the Jack. If Diamonds is your weak link and you're going to have to lose the lead a couple of times before you can build enough winners, a hold-up may work very well. But if some other suit is far more threatening, grab the trick before the opponents change their minds!

PRESERVING AN ENTRY

When entries to the hand with the long suit are in short supply, special care may be needed:

WEST (DECLARER)	EAST (DUMMY)
♠ A K 3	♠ 6 5 2
♡ A K 5	♡ 9 8 3
◇ 8 4 3	◇ A K 7 6 2
♣ A J 7 5	♣ 4 2

WEST	EAST
1 ♣	1 ◇
2 NT	3 NT
Pass	

The opening lead is a Spade, and you win with the King. You've got five top tricks and need only a 3–2 Diamond split to score four winners in that suit, but you must watch your entries! If you cash the two top Diamonds and play a third round, the opponents will win the trick—and you won't be able to get back to dummy until the next deal.

The right plan is to lose the *first* Diamond trick instead of the third one. At trick two, play a small Diamond from both hands! When you regain the lead, cash the Ace of Diamonds. If both opponents follow suit, you're home; the King will extract the last enemy Diamond *and the lead will be in dummy,* so you'll be able to cash the two length winners and just make your game contract.

SUIT PLAY

Drawing Trumps

So long as there aren't any emergencies, try to draw the enemy trumps as soon as possible. For example:

WEST (DECLARER)	EAST (DUMMY)
♠ A 10 3	♠ K Q 6
♡ A K J 3 2	♡ Q 10 7 4
◇ 8 7 4	◇ K Q J 3
♣ 10 6	♣ 5 3

WEST	EAST
1 ♡	3 ♡
4 ♡	Pass

North cashes the King and Ace of Clubs and switches to a Spade. When you declare a suit contract, count your probable *winners* and probable *losers*. You have eight certain winners in the major suits and can readily promote the additional two tricks that you need in Diamonds, and there are only three losers (two Club tricks and the Diamond Ace). This analysis reveals that your contract is assured so long as the opponents don't score a fatal ruff, so win the Spade lead in whichever hand you please and draw all of the enemy trumps. (You'll need to play two rounds if trumps split 2–2, three rounds if they divide 3–1, and four rounds if they happen to be 4–0, so keep a careful *count* as you go along.) Then stop! You've got to keep at least one trump in order to prevent a fiasco in the Club suit, so turn your attention to Diamonds and drive out the enemy Ace.

WHEN NOT TO DRAW TRUMPS

The quick discard. If your checkup of winners and losers indicates that you have too many potential losers, and you can't draw trumps without losing the lead, a quick discard may save the day. An example of this useful technique was provided in Bridge Movie 3.

Ruffing losers in dummy. Another good time to postpone drawing trumps is when you desperately need dummy's supply for ruffing purposes:

WEST (DECLARER)   EAST (DUMMY)

♠ A K Q 10 9   ♠ J 3 2
♡ K 7   ♡ A 8 5 3 2
◇ A 8 6   ◇ 5
♣ J 4 3   ♣ 9 8 5 2

WEST	EAST
1 ♠	2 ♠
4 ♠	Pass

North wins the first three tricks by leading out the King, Ace, and Queen of Clubs; South plays small Clubs on the first two rounds and then discards a small Heart. North persists with the Ten of Clubs, dummy follows with the Nine, South discards a small Diamond, and you ruff with the Nine of Spades.

You need the rest of the tricks to make your contract and drawing trumps will leave you with two losers in Diamonds, so it's time to shop around for a better idea. The right plan is to cash the Ace of Diamonds, lead a small Diamond and ruff it with dummy's Two of Spades, reenter your hand by leading the Three of Spades to one of your honors, and ruff your last losing Diamond with the Jack of Spades. Now return to your hand by leading a low Heart to your King and draw the enemy trumps.

The crossruff. On occasion, it may be necessary to eliminate drawing trumps entirely because extensive ruffing is required in both hands:

WEST (DECLARER)	EAST (DUMMY)
♠ 8 6 5 4	♠ A
♡ A Q J 7	♡ K 10 9 8
◇ 7	◇ A J 5 3
♣ 9 8 6 5	♣ 7 4 3 2

WEST	EAST
Pass	1 ◇
1 ♡	2 ♡
Pass	

North leads a Spade, and dummy's Ace wins. If you lead out all your trumps, you'll wind up with only six tricks. Instead, cash the Ace of Diamonds and ruff a Diamond in your hand, trump a Spade in dummy, ruff another Diamond in your hand, and continue to **crossruff** back and forth for as long as you can. This clever plan ultimately produces nine winners, enabling you to land your contract with an overtrick.

Handling a bad trump split. If one opponent turns up with a huge number of trumps, you may have to delay drawing them in order to avoid exhausting your own supply:

NORTH
♠ K J 7 5
♡ J 4
◊ 10 8 3
♣ A J 10 9

SOUTH
♠ A Q 6 3
♡ 6 3 2
◊ K Q J
♣ K Q 2

SOUTH	NORTH
1 NT	2 ♣
2 ♠	4 ♠
Pass	

West leads the Eight of Clubs, and you win and cash the King and Jack of Spades. If trumps split 3–2, draw the last one and drive out the Ace of Diamonds. A Heart return won't bother you, for dummy's remaining trump will prevent more than two losers in that suit.

Now suppose that one opponent discards on the second round of Spades, thereby informing you that trumps have divided 4–1. If you draw them all, you'll use up your own supply; and when you then turn to the Diamonds, the opponents will defeat you by taking their Ace and cashing three or four Heart tricks. Therefore, stop drawing trumps and drive out the Ace of Diamonds right now— while dummy can still guard the Heart department. When you regain the lead, finish drawing trumps and rattle off your winners. The complete deal:

NORTH
♠ K J 7 5
♡ J 4
◇ 10 8 3
♣ A J 10 9

WEST
♠ 10 8 4 2
♡ A Q 8 5
◇ A 7 5
♣ 8 7

EAST
♠ 9
♡ K 10 9 7
◇ 9 6 4 2
♣ 6 5 4 3

SOUTH
♠ A Q 6 3
♡ 6 3 2
◇ K Q J
♣ K Q 2

RUFFING OUT A SUIT

Trump Power can also be used to establish some length winners without losing any tricks in the process:

NORTH
♠ 7 2
♡ 5 4 2
◇ A 6
♣ A K 9 7 6 3

WEST
♠ 9 6 5 3
♡ K Q J
◇ K 7 5 2
♣ J 4

EAST
♠ 8 4
♡ 10 9 8
◇ J 10 9 8 3
♣ Q 10 5

SOUTH
♠ A K Q J 10
♡ A 7 6 3
◇ Q 4
♣ 8 2

As the result of a bidding misunderstanding, you wind up in a risky Six Spade contract. West leads the King of Hearts, and you win with the Ace and draw trumps in four rounds (discarding two Hearts from dummy). Is there a way to bring home your slam?

The opponents are thirsting to cash two Heart tricks, so you must try to establish dummy's Clubs without allowing them to gain the lead. The right plan is to cash the Ace and King of Clubs and ruff the third round of Clubs with your last trump. Thanks to the 3–2 split, the rest of the Clubs are good; so enter dummy with the Diamond Ace and cash the three length winners. Then score up a result that should have the opponents grumbling to themselves for the rest of the evening! (And don't forget your 150 honors!) *

THE ART OF DEDUCTION

The renowned Sherlock Holmes once puzzled an erstwhile police inspector by calling attention to the fact that a dog did nothing in the nighttime. This actually turned out to be a vital clue, since the animal's failure to bark showed that the criminal was someone it knew quite well. Holmes would have had little trouble with the following deal:

NORTH
♠ A 5 2
♡ 8 7 3
◇ Q 5
♣ A K Q 9 4

SOUTH
♠ K Q 3
♡ A Q J 9 5 2
◇ 10 6 4
♣ 3

* Technical note for sharp-eyed readers: The weird-looking opening lead of the King of Diamonds doesn't beat the slam, even though it drives out dummy's side entry. Win with the Ace, play four rounds of trumps, and use the entry-preserving play of ducking the first round of Clubs in both hands!

The bidding:

SOUTH	WEST	NORTH	EAST
—	—	—	Pass
1 ♡	Pass	2 ♣	2 ◇
2 ♡	Pass	4 ♡	Pass
Pass	Pass		

West leads the Nine of Diamonds, and East tops dummy's Queen with the King. East now cashes the Ace of Diamonds, West playing the deuce, and continues with the Diamond Jack. The reason for this apparently strange play becomes clear when West ruffs with the Ten of Hearts! Dummy cannot overruff, and so discards the Four of Clubs. West now exits with a Spade, and you must avoid losing a trick to the King of Hearts in order to make your contract.

There are three trumps still outstanding, and the normal play when missing three or more trumps including the King is to finesse. However, circumstances are far from normal! East may not be a canine, but his silence at his first turn to bid is a clue worthy of attention. The play to the first three tricks shows that West began with a small doubleton Diamond, so East must have started with six Diamonds headed by the A K J. If he also held the King of Hearts, he surely would have opened the bidding. So West must hold the missing monarch, and your only chance is that his previous ruff has left it unprotected. You properly lay down the Ace of Hearts and are amply rewarded when West drops the King, the full deal being:

NORTH
♠ A 5 2
♡ 8 7 3
◇ Q 5
♣ A K Q 9 4

WEST
♠ J 9 7 6 4
♡ K 10
◇ 9 2
♣ J 10 8 5

EAST
♠ 10 8
♡ 6 4
◇ A K J 8 7 3
♣ 7 6 2

SOUTH
♠ K Q 3
♡ A Q J 9 5 2
◇ 10 6 4
♣ 3

If East had opened the bidding with One Diamond, you would play him for the King of Hearts and take the finesse. As Holmes would say, "Elementary, my dear reader!"

BRIDGE MOVIE 4: DANGER IN THE WEST

You are South, and deal yourself the following hand:

♠ A 6 2
♡ Q 7 5
◇ 5 4 2
♣ A K J 10

What call do you make?

ANSWER: One Club. You're not strong enough to open with One Notrump (14 HCP) and your longest suit is four cards, so bid your longer minor.

West passes, North bids One Diamond, and East passes. *Now what do you bid?*

ANSWER: One Notrump. Partner's response is unlimited, so you don't have enough information to take charge of the auction. Instead, share information by showing that your hand is balanced and worth precisely 13–15 points.

West passes, North bids Three Notrump, and East passes. *What call do you make?*

ANSWER: Pass. Partner has announced that game should be reached and slam is out of the question, and you must respect his signoff.

West also passes, bringing the auction to a close, and leads the Five of Spades. Partner puts down this dummy:

NORTH

♠ J 10
♡ A K 2
◇ A Q J 10 6
♣ 7 6 4

Opening   *How do you like your con-*
Lead: ♠ 5   *tract?*

SOUTH

♠ A 6 2
♡ Q 7 5
◇ 5 4 2
♣ A K J 10

ANSWER: You have seven power winners and there's an excellent chance to develop two more tricks, so you're a favorite to make it. But first you must do something to foil your pesky opponents, who have unobligingly struck at your weakest link.

You play dummy's Ten of Spades and East covers with the Spade King. *What do you play from your hand?*

ANSWER: The Two of Spades. You have only one Spade stopper and no weaker suit elsewhere, so try to destroy the enemy's communications by holding up your Ace.

NORTH

♠ J
♡ A K 2
◇ A Q J 10 6
♣ 7 6 4

Lead: ♠ 8

SOUTH

♠ A 6
♡ Q 7 5
◇ 5 4 2
♣ A K J 10

East returns the Eight of Spades. *Now what?*

ANSWER: Continue your hold-up by playing the Six of Spades. West produces the Spade Queen, winning the trick, and fires back the Three of Spades. You discard dummy's Four of Clubs, East discards the Three of Hearts, and you must now take your Spade Ace.

NORTH

♠ —
♡ A K 2
◇ A Q J 10 6
♣ 7 6

SOUTH

♠ —
♡ Q 7 5
◇ 5 4 2
♣ A K J 10

How do you proceed from here?

ANSWER: Lead a small Diamond and finesse the Queen (or Jack, or Ten) if West plays low. Losing the lead to East won't hurt, since he is now out of Spades, so try to build the additional winners that you need by taking the Diamond finesse.

You lead the Two of Diamonds, West plays the Diamond Three, you finesse dummy's Queen, and East plays the Seven of Diamonds. The position now is:

NORTH

♠ —
♡ A K 2
◇ A J 10 6
♣ 7 6

SOUTH

♠ —
♡ Q 7 5
◇ 5 4
♣ A K J 10

Should you take the Club finesse? If not, what is the right play?

ANSWER: No! Losing the lead to *West* will be fatal, since he still owns a vast number of Spades (in fact, enough to defeat your contract!). West is therefore the *danger hand* and you must prevent him from gaining the lead, so re-enter your hand in Hearts or Clubs and repeat the Diamond finesse.

You lead dummy's Two of Hearts, East plays the Heart Eight, you put up your Queen, and West follows with the Four of Hearts. You now lead the Four of Diamonds, West plays the Eight of Diamonds, you finesse dummy's

Jack, and East produces the King. (The defenders are also allowed to use the hold-up play!) The situation is now:

NORTH

♠ —
♡ A K
◇ A 10 6
♣ 7 6

♣ 2 led

SOUTH

♠ —
♡ 7 5
◇ 5
♣ A K J 10

East returns the Two of Clubs. *What is your plan for the remaining tricks?*

ANSWER: Put up the Club Ace (or King), lead a Diamond to one of dummy's honors to extract the last enemy Diamond, cash dummy's two length winners in Diamonds and discard your Ten and Jack of Clubs, and win the rest of the tricks with the top Hearts and Club King. West's established Spades go down the drain, and you bring home your contract with an overtrick The complete deal:

NORTH
♠ J 10
♡ A K 2
◇ A Q J 10 6
♣ 7 6 4

WEST
♠ Q 9 7 5 4 3
♡ 6 4
◇ 8 3
♣ Q 8 5

EAST
♠ K 8
♡ J 10 9 8 3
◇ K 9 7
♣ 9 3 2

SOUTH
♠ A 6 2
♡ Q 7 5
◇ 5 4 2
♣ A K J 10

The bidding:

SOUTH	WEST	NORTH	EAST
1 ♣	Pass	1 ◇	Pass
1 NT	Pass	3 NT	Pass
Pass	Pass		

East cleverly gave you a chance to go wrong by with-holding his King of Diamonds the first time around. If you had fallen into his trap and taken the Club finesse, West would have won with the Queen and cashed enough Spade winners to defeat your contract by two tricks! And the Diamond finesse strategy also ensures your contract if West has the missing King, since it brings home the suit without allowing him to gain the lead and make a thorough nuisance of himself by running the Spades.

5

Defensive Bidding and Play

Wise bridge players, like knowledgeable sports fans, value and appreciate good defense. Declarer gets to see his partner's hand before deciding on his plan of action, but the defenders start off totally ignorant of each other's holdings. Therefore, you're going to need good teamwork as well as card skill in order to defend effectively.

THE OPENING LEAD

To partially offset the advantage of declarer's superior firepower, the defenders get to strike first by making the opening lead. This is the only play made without the aid of seeing the dummy, so keen judgment is required—plus a favorable nod from lady luck.

CHOOSING THE CARD

The card that you select for your opening lead serves two important purposes. First, it should help your side's *trick-taking potential* without doing declarer any great favors. In addition, the card should *inform your partner* about your holding in the suit so that he can cooperate intelligently in the defense.

For example, suppose you decide to lead from K Q J 3. The Three-spot would be a terrible choice, since it hands declarer an extra trick if he has A 10 and gains absolutely nothing in return, so you must lead one of your honors. Since they are equivalent in power, the only remaining consideration is to let partner know what you have; and the customary procedure is to lead *the top card from an honor sequence* (except for suits headed by A K, from which the King is led). Other important examples of the right card to lead, once you have decided on the suit, are summarized in Table 5 on page 170.

CHOOSING THE SUIT

Opening leads are difficult even for experts, so don't expect to make the right choice every time. Here are some helpful guidelines:

1. Remember that your goal is to defeat the enemy contract. Be careful not to part with your power winners too soon:

YOU (WEST) HOLD:	NORTH	SOUTH
♠ A 4 2	—	1 ♡
♡ 7 3 2	3 ♡	4 ♡
◇ J 6 5	Pass	
♣ K Q J 6		

Leading the Ace of Spades may actually help declarer

TABLE 5. OPENING LEADS: SOME TYPICAL CARD CHOICES

Holding in Suit	vs. Notrump	vs. Suits
TWO-CARD SUITS		
Any	Top card	Top card
THREE-CARD SUITS		
987 or worse	Top card	Top card
10xx, Jxx, Qxx, Kxx	3rd best	3rd best
Q10x, K10x, KJx	3rd best	3rd best
109x, J10x, QJx, KQx	Top card	Top card
Axx	3rd best	Ace
AKx or better	King	King
FOUR-CARD OR LONGER SUITS		
9876 or worse	4th best	4th best
10xxx, Jxxx, Qxxx, Q10xx	4th best	4th best
1097x, J108x, QJ9x	Top card*	Top card
1098x, J109x, QJ10x	Top card	Top card
Q1098	Ten	Ten
Kxxx, K10xx, KJxx	4th best	4th best
K1098, KJ109	2nd best	2nd best
KQxx	4th best	King
KQ10x, KQJx	King	King
Axxx, A10xx, AJxx, AQxx	4th best	Ace
A1098, AJ109	2nd best	2nd best
AKxx	4th best	King
AKJx or better	King**	King

* See footnotes on opposite page.

by turning his King into a sure winner. You need *four* tricks to beat this contract, so start developing them by leading the King of Clubs.

2. *Usually, try to build length winners against No-trump games and partials.* A declarer at Notrump usually owns a majority of the high cards, so try to make the most of your small ones by building some length winners. A *five-card or longer* suit is an excellent place to begin:

SUIT	LEAD
K Q J 10 3	King
A K 7 3 2	Three
A Q 6 5 2	Five
K J 8 6 3 2	Six

When you don't have a solid sequence, a small card is led in order to preserve the honors for use as entries later on; and the *fourth best* card is chosen to help part-ner determine your length in the suit. (When you later play an even smaller card, he'll know that you began with at least a five-bagger.) You're quite willing to let de-clarer score one possibly undeserved trick with a Queen or King, for you are likely to build three or four tricks in return. In fact, the only times when you should refuse to lead from a five-card or longer suit against a Notrump contract are: (a) the opponents have bid it, indicating that

* From a *five-card or six-card* suit, lead fourth best unless you have 10976, J1087, or QJ98.
** From a *five-card or six-card* suit, lead fourth best unless you have AKJ9, AKJ10, or AKQ.

you'd better look elsewhere for tricks unless your holding in the suit is super-solid;* (b) partner has bid a different suit, and yours isn't outstanding enough for you to overrule his suggestion; or (c) your suit is very weak and you have no probable outside entries, so you can't gain the lead to run your length winners even if they do become established.

If you don't have an acceptable five-card or longer suit, a solid or nearly solid four-carder is likely to be a good choice. For example, lead the Queen from Q J 10 7 or the Jack from J 10 9 8; this should build a trick or two without helping declarer. Leading the Four-spot from Q 10 7 4 is also reasonable if the suit has not been bid by the enemy. However, avoid a four-card holding such as A Q 3 2. You're likely to give away a trick to declarer's King, and you'll probably get nothing in return because your potential for length winners is so poor. One good alternative is to try and hit a long suit in *partner's* hand, and experience has shown that leading from an *unbid three-card major* is often an excellent shot. Another possibility is to opt for safety by leading from three or four small cards in an unbid suit; if partner's honors are captured by declarer, they probably could have been finessed anyway.

3. *Usually, don't underlead a side-suit Ace or King-Queen against a suit contract.* Trying to build length winners against a *suit* contract is probably futile, for declarer can simply ruff as soon as he runs out of the suit. There-

---

* But don't be faked out by an artificial bid! A Stayman Two Club response doesn't promise any strength or length in the bid suit, so there is no reason to be deterred from a normal Club lead.

fore, avoid holdings like A Q 6 5 2; if you blow a trick to declarer's King, you'll almost surely wind up with a net loss. A suit like A K 7 3 2 *is* a good place to begin the attack, but be careful to lead the King and ensure a trick or two before a pestiferous trump appears on the scene. Solid sequences like A K Q J or Q J 10 9 are frequently very desirable, since you can build some winners without giving declarer any help. Leading the King from K Q 9 5 3 is also reasonable, but involves more risk.

Against a suit contract, the lead of a side-suit singleton is often a fine way to turn the dreaded ruffing power against the enemy. You need some excess low trumps for this to work, and partner must be able to gain the lead so that he can give you a ruff or two. However, avoid leading a singleton King or Queen; declarer may well lose a trick to your honor if left to his own devices. Finally, if most of your alternatives are too risky, lead from a number of small cards in a unbid suit or in trumps.

4 *Usually, play safe against a slam contract unless you see a probable route to a set.* You only need two tricks to defeat a Six Notrump contract, so there's no need to try and build length winners. Therefore, *don't* risk giving declarer any undeserved tricks! Reject any suit containing some honors, lead from a suit consisting of several small cards, and let him do his own work. However, it's quite proper to attack when you can see a probable set. *Do* lead the top of a solid sequence like K Q J, lead the King from K Q x *if* you also have an Ace in a different suit, and by all means cash two Aces or an A K in the same suit.

Against a suit slam, also attack if you see two probable

tricks. Cashing an Ace in an *unbid* suit may be right, especially when you have a probable winner elsewhere or when the enemy auction warns that you're in danger of losing your Ace to some quick discards. However, don't help declarer develop winners by leading Aces in suits bid by his side; try to build a second trick for your own team. Even leading small from Q x x in an unbid suit may be justified, hoping that partner has the King. If the opponents reach a grand slam in a suit, leading from a few small trumps is likely to be both safe and effective.

5. *Listen closely to the bidding.* Tend to lead a suit partner has bid unless you have an excellent reason to do otherwise, and usually avoid suits bid by the enemy. Also keep a keen ear tuned to the enemy auction, and try to deduce their probable holdings:

YOU (WEST) HOLD:	NORTH	SOUTH
♠ A Q 10 3	—	1 ♠
♡ 7 6 3	1 NT	2 ♡
◇ 8 5 2	3 ♡	4 ♡
♣ J 10 9	Pass	

Dummy is likely to be short in Spades because he preferred South's second suit, so your Spade honors are in great danger of being ruffed away. Therefore, lead a Heart and try to draw dummy's trumps.

The bidding may also turn an apparently unattractive lead into a mandatory choice:

YOU (WEST) HOLD:	NORTH	SOUTH
♠ K 4	—	1 ♠
♡ J 10 8 7	2 ◊	2 ♡
◊ 9 6 5 3	3 ◊	3 ♠
♣ K 10 2	4 ♠	Pass

Leading away from K x x is usually poor strategy, for you're likely to blow your only trick in the suit if declarer's side turns up with both the Ace and Queen. In this situation, however, the right lead is the Two of Clubs! Dummy has promised a lot of good Diamonds that may provide valuable discards, declarer has announced strength in Hearts, and neither opponent has mentioned Clubs (or promised Club strength indirectly by bidding Notrump). Here's the complete deal:

NORTH
♠ 9 7
♡ Q 2
◊ A K Q 7 4 2
♣ 9 6 4

WEST (YOU)
♠ K 4
♡ J 10 8 7
◊ 9 6 5 3
♣ K 10 2

EAST (PARTNER)
♠ 6 5 2
♡ 9 6 4
◊ J 10 8
♣ A J 7 5

SOUTH
♠ A Q J 10 8 3
♡ A K 5 3
◊ —
♣ Q 8 3

If you lead a red suit, declarer quickly throws away his Clubs on dummy's top Diamonds and easily makes his contract. But after your inspired Club lead, partner takes his Ace and fires back a Club through declarer's Queen, and you cash two more winners. Now declarer will cry bitterly when the Spade finesse loses, for his contract will be defeated. Moral: Good opening leads often make for unlucky declarers!

SIGNALLING

It is strictly illegal to smile broadly or nod when partner leads a suit that you like, or to frown menacingly when you don't care much for his selection. Fortunately, there is a permissible (and effective!) way of sending these important messages:

DUMMY

◇ 6 5 3

PARTNER   YOU

◇ A K J 7   ◇ ? 8 2

DECLARER

◇ ? 9 4

Partner properly leads the King of Diamonds, but then runs into a terrible predicament. If Declarer has the Queen of Diamonds, a continuation will present him with an undeserved winner in the suit; but if you have the Queen, he definitely wants to cash three fast winners.

Without some help from you, this problem is completely insoluble. From Q 8 2, you should play your *Eight-spot;* this *unnecessarily high spot card* asks partner to continue leading the suit. With 10 8 2, however, make your normal play of the deuce. A *low spot card* is a warning signal, and partner is advised not to persist unless he has a good reason (such as A K Q).

To be sure, this method is not infallible. With 10 9 8, you must play the apparently high Eight-spot in order to discourage a continuation; while with Q 3 2, you've got to signal with a feeble Three-spot and hope partner gets the message. But it will work most of the time, and signalling is essential for several reasons:

1. It helps the defenders lead the right suits. Signals help your side attack declarer's weakest link, and keep away from leads that will help him out. Note that you can also signal when making a discard: An unnecessarily high spot card informs partner that you'd appreciate the lead of that suit if he ever gets in, while a low spot suggests that he look elsewhere for tricks.

2. It helps the defenders keep the right suits. A declarer in trouble may run a long suit and hope for a mistake, and signalling will enable your side to guard the right suits. If a defender's first discard in a particular suit is an unnecessarily high spot card, he plans to protect that suit and wants his partner to guard something else. But if the first discard in a given suit is a low spot, he is weak in that suit and is asking partner to protect it as best he can.

3. It helps the defenders get ruffs. Suppose partner leads a side-suit King against a suit contract and dummy turns up with Q 7 4. If you have a doubleton, partner should cash his Ace and give you a ruff before declarer can draw trumps. But if he plays his Ace and you happen to have a lot of cards in this suit, *declarer* may ruff and obtain a useful discard on dummy's promoted Queen. The solution is to signal high with a doubleton (for example, play the Eight-spot from 8 2), but play small with three or more low cards.

Signalling is the only legal way to exchange information during the defense. In fact, it is so important that expert defenders assign some meaning to just about every play that they make!

DEFENSIVE STRATEGY

LEADING TO SUBSEQUENT TRICKS

When leading to a trick other than the first one, tend to follow the opening lead guidelines—but keep these exceptions in mind:

1. Remember that you and your partner are on the same team. Don't base your plans solely on your own hand! Study the dummy, and pay very close attention to partner's plays. If he appears to have an important goal, such as building length winners in his suit or drawing dummy's trumps, cooperate by playing back the suit he has led unless you have an extremely good reason to overrule him.

2. When returning your partner's suit, give him the count. Partner often needs to know how many cards you have in a suit that he has led, and you can let him know by handling your spot cards carefully:

DUMMY

♣ 8

PARTNER   YOU

♣ A J 9 7 4   (a) ♣ K 6 5   *or*

                                     (b) ♣ K 6 5 3

DECLARER

?

Partner leads the Seven of Clubs against declarer's Three Notrump contract, you win with the King, and declarer plays the deuce. You return a Club, declarer puts up the Ten, and partner captures it with his Jack.

If partner now cashes his Ace and you began with holding (a), declarer (who started with Q 10 3 2) will happily play his Three-spot and score an undeserved trick with the Queen later on. To prevent this, partner must shift suits and wait for you to lead through declarer once again. But if you started with holding (b), declarer's Queen is now all alone; and partner can run the whole suit (and beat the contract!) by laying down his Ace. Therefore, you should *give partner the count* when you lead to the second trick. Here's how:

YOUR HOLDING IN PARTNER'S SUIT	CORRECT CARD TO RETURN
Two or three cards, or a suit that is now headed by a sequence of honors	Highest remaining card
Four or more cards (but no honor sequence)	Original fourth best

Thus, return the Six of Clubs in example (a) but lead the Three-spot in case (b). This will keep partner from suffering a nervous breakdown—and, even more importantly, from making the wrong play.

3. *When starting a new suit, warn partner not to return it if your holding is very weak.* Here's another situation that requires good teamwork:

DUMMY

♠ 6 3

PARTNER   YOU

♠ K J 7   (a) ♠ 9 8 5 4 2

or

(b) ♠ A 9 8 4 2

DECLARER

?

Once again, you are trying to stop declarer from bringing home a Three Notrump contract. Partner's opening Club lead turned out to be a total disaster (dummy showed up with A K J 10), so you decide to attack Spades when you gain the lead. You play a spot card, declarer tries the Ten, and partner grabs it with his Jack.

If you have holding (a), a Spade return will run right into declarer's A Q—and blow a trick. But if you own suit (b), partner can defeat the contract by cashing the King and playing another Spade! In example (a), therefore, reject the normal Notrump play of fourth best and lead the *Nine-spot* at trick two ("top of nothing"). This high spot denies possession of an honor, and warns partner not to return the suit if his own holding is shaky. In case (b), however, make your normal lead of the Four of Spades.

4. If dummy is on your right, tend to lead its weak suits. If you're in doubt as to which suit to attack, *leading up to weakness* is likely to be a good choice. In the preceding example (b), a Spade lead is perfectly safe because dummy is so weak; at worst, declarer will put up the King and win a finesse that he could just as easily have taken by himself. However, the Spade lead is more dangerous if dummy is on your *left,* since declarer's finesse will now lose so long as you just leave the Spade suit alone. In such instances, follow this guideline:

5. When in doubt, play safe unless dummy indicates that you must take tricks in a hurry. If nothing alarming is about to happen, it's usually best to avoid giving declarer any gifts:

NORTH (DUMMY)
♠ J 7 6 3 2
♡ K 4
◇ Q 3 2
♣ 6 4 3

WEST (YOU)
♠ A 5
♡ Q J 10 7
◇ K 10 5
♣ J 8 7 2

EAST (PARTNER)
?

SOUTH (DECLARER)
?

The bidding:

SOUTH	WEST	NORTH	EAST
1 ♠	Pass	2 ♠	Pass
4 ♠	Pass	Pass	Pass

You lead the Queen of Hearts and dummy's King wins, partner playing the deuce and declarer the Three-spot. Declarer now leads a small Spade from dummy and puts up the King, partner playing the Four of Spades, and you take your Ace. Leading a Diamond could easily blow a trick, and there is no emergency; dummy does not have any long suits on which declarer can discard his losers, and your high cards will clearly prevent South from using suits of his own to discard any of dummy's small cards. Therefore, adopt a **passive defense**; get off lead safely by playing the Jack of Hearts or a Spade and let declarer do his own work. His hand:

♠ K Q 10 9 8
♡ A 3
◇ J 6 4
♣ A K Q

If you lead a Diamond, declarer simply plays small from dummy and must get a trick in the suit; but after your safe exit, he will have to lose three Diamond tricks —and his contract.

The following situation, however, requires a different strategy:

NORTH (DUMMY)
♠ J 7 6
♡ K 4
◇ Q 3 2
♣ A K Q J 9

WEST (YOU)   EAST (PARTNER)
♠ 5 4   ?
♡ Q J 10 7 3
◇ K 10 5
♣ 10 6 5

SOUTH (DECLARER)
?

The bidding:

SOUTH	WEST	NORTH	EAST
—	—	1 NT	Pass
4 ♠	Pass	Pass	Pass

You lead the Queen of Hearts once again, but this time partner tops dummy's King with the Ace. He returns the deuce of Hearts, and your Jack wins the trick. Dummy's awesome Club suit will surely provide discards for any losers that declarer may have, so an **active defense** is mandatory. Lead the Five of Diamonds! Here's the complete deal:

NORTH
♠ J 7 6
♡ K 4
◇ Q 3 2
♣ A K Q J 9

WEST (YOU)
♠ 5 4
♡ Q J 10 7 3
◇ K 10 5
♣ 10 6 5

EAST (PARTNER)
♠ 3 2
♡ A 9 6 2
◇ A 9 8 7
♣ 7 3 2

SOUTH
♠ A K Q 10 9 8
♡ 8 5
◇ J 6 4
♣ 8 4

Your Diamond return enables the defense to score two fast winners and beat the contract before declarer can get in to run his tricks. And it costs nothing even if South does have the Ace, for he would have been able to sluff all his Diamond losers anyway.

If declarer should play a low Heart from dummy at trick one and you then lead another Heart to partner's Ace, he should also appreciate the need to take tricks in a hurry and lay down his Ace of Diamonds. You *signal* great enthusiasm by playing the Ten, and he continues Diamonds to defeat the contract.

DEFENSE IN SECOND POSITION

If declarer or dummy leads a *spot card* and you are next

to play, you should usually play *low* ("second hand low"). Preserving an honor may enable you to capture an enemy honor later on, or you may cause declarer to misguess. However, *do* play high if: (a) you have a solid sequence like K Q J or Q J 10; (b) you can win the trick and then cash enough winners to defeat the contract; or (c) an emergency situation exists—you must take your trick now or never get it, or your side needs the lead right away.

If declarer or dummy leads an *honor*, it is often correct to **cover** with a higher one—but not always! Let's look at some examples:

DUMMY

♡ Q 7

PARTNER   YOU

?   (a) ♡ K 10 9

or

(b) ♡ K 3 2

DECLARER

?

If dummy's Queen is led, you should cover with the King in either case. Playing low will give declarer three tricks if he has A J 4, for he'll let the Queen ride and then finesse the Jack next time; but when you cover, the third round of the suit will be won by the promoted Ten of Hearts (yours in example a, partner's in case b).

The following situation, however, is different:

DUMMY

(a) ♡ Q J 10 9 *or*
(b) ♡ Q J 9

PARTNER   YOU

?   ♡ K 5 3 2

DECLARER

?

When dummy's Queen is led in example (a), you should refuse to cover. Your side cannot possibly have any high cards to promote in view of dummy's solid sequence, and playing your King will give declarer four tricks instead of three if he has A 6 4. Therefore, play low and continue to duck if more honors are led from dummy.

Also decline to cover the Queen in example (b). Covering blows a trick if declarer has A x or A x x, for he can avoid any Heart losers by finessing dummy's Nine-spot on the way back. However, *do* cover when dummy's second honor is led. Now that there is no finesse position remaining, driving out declarer's Ace will promote a trick for your side if partner owns the Ten.

To avoid confusion (and lost tricks), keep this guideline in mind: If you can *safely wait and cover an equal honor next time,* or if you deduce that there is *nothing to promote* in either your hand or partner's, *don't cover.* Otherwise, you should usually "cover an honor with an honor."

DEFENSE IN THIRD POSITION

If partner leads a small card and you are able to top dummy's offering, your normal play is to fight for the trick by playing your *highest* card ("third hand high"):

DUMMY

◇ 8 4 2

PARTNER   YOU

◇ 6 led   ◇ K 10 3

DECLARER

?

Partner leads the Six of Diamonds and dummy plays small, and the right play is the King. If you erroneously choose the Ten, you'll give away a trick if declarer began with A J 5 or (at a Notrump contract when partner could be underleading the Ace) Q 9 5. However, watch out for these exceptions: (a) Play the *lowest of equal honors,* such as the Queen from K Q 3 or the Ten from Q J 10 3. This does not reduce your chances to win the trick, and helps partner figure out what you have in the suit. (b) If dummy has an honor, it is frequently correct to *finesse against the dummy:*

DUMMY

◇ J 4 2

PARTNER   YOU

◇ 5 led   ◇ K 10 3

DECLARER

?

If partner leads the Diamond Five and dummy plays low, put in the Ten and preserve your King to cover dummy's Jack later on. This plan saves a trick if declarer has A 7 6 or A 7, and costs nothing if declarer has only the Queen because he was assured of one winner anyway. Similar reasoning applies if dummy has Q 4 2 and you hold K J 3 (insert the Jack if dummy plays small), or if dummy has K 4 2 and you have A J 10 3 (play the Ten). If dummy's honor is played, however, you should definitely cover.

BIDDING AFTER THE OPPONENTS OPEN

Caution is clearly indicated when the opponents open the bidding, for they could easily own the balance of power. If your hand is strong enough, however, your best defense may be a good offense.

THE OVERCALL

Suit overcalls. If your right-hand opponent opens with one of a suit, you need about 9 to 17 points and a good five-card or longer suit in order to bid (**overcall**) at the *one-level*. And to venture forth at the *two-level*, your suit must be truly impressive.

For example, suppose that the opponent on your right deals and opens with One Diamond, and you hold any of these hands:

(a) ♠ A Q 8 6 5   (b) ♠ Q 4 2
    ♡ K 6 3   ♡ K 6 3
    ◇ 7 4   ◇ 7 4
    ♣ 10 8 7   ♣ A Q 8 6 5

(c) ♠ 10 5
    ♡ A 6 4
    ◇ 7 4
    ♣ A Q J 8 6 3

Hand (a) is a minimum One Spade overcall. This suit is too weak to bid at the two-level, however, so you must pass with hand (b) even though you have somewhat more strength. A Two Club overcall would show a fine suit and some outside strength, as in hand (c).

Overcalls at the three-level and four-level are pre-emptive, similar to the corresponding opening bids. A *single jump overcall* shows 18 or more points in standard bidding (and a fine suit), but is better used as pre-emptive (similar to a weak two-bid).

The One Notrump overcall. An overcall of One Notrump is similar to a One Notrump opening bid, showing 16 to 18 HCP and a balanced hand. However, it absolutely guarantees some stoppers in the suit bid by the enemy, since that is where they are likely to begin their attack.

THE TAKEOUT DOUBLE

Sometimes you'll have enough strength to compete over the enemy opening of one of a suit, but will need partner's assistance in selecting the best suit for your side. Suppose your right-hand opponent opens with One Diamond and you hold either of these hands:

(a) ♠ K Q 6 3   (b) ♠ A 10 6 5
    ♡ A J 6 2   ♡ A Q 9 4
    ◇ 7   ◇ —
    ♣ K J 10 4   ♣ Q 8 6 4 3

None of your suits is strong enough for an overcall, but passing would be distinctly cowardly. To resolve this dilemma, the standard procedure is to *double*. The double of an opening bid of one of a suit is *not* an attempt to penalize the opponents; a seven-trick contract is just too hard to defeat. Instead, this call is used to let partner know that you have *a hand worth at least an opening bid and fine support for all unbid suits,* and it asks him to pick the one that he likes best. He is under strict orders *not* to pass unless he has a long and completely solid holding, such as K Q J 10 5, in the enemy suit. His replies are:

RESPONSE TO TAKEOUT DOUBLE	MEANING
New suit bid without jumping	0–8 points, 3-card or longer suit.
Jump in new suit	9–11 points, *not* forcing, usually a good 4-card or longer suit.
Cue-bid of enemy suit	12 or more points, *forcing.*
One Notrump	7–10 HCP, stoppers in enemy suit, balanced hand.
Two Notrump	11–13 HCP, stoppers in enemy suit, balanced hand.

The invaluable **takeout double** allows you and your partner to contest the auction while keeping the bidding at a low level—and your side out of serious trouble. If your right-hand opponent opens with One Club, One Heart, or One Spade, however, you must *pass* with hands (a) and (b). You cannot double with such poor support for the unbid Diamond suit, and your suits are too weak for an overcall.

AFTERWORD

Congratulations! You are now a bridge player. There's a great deal more to this best of all card games, however, so let's conclude with some tips for improving your technique.

BRIDGE PSYCHOLOGY

Bridge is a challenging game, and you must expect to make a fair number of mistakes. Don't try to hide them (or, even worse, blame them on your partner!); study them carefully so that you can learn where you went wrong. And when partner goofs, *don't* read him the riot act! He'll probably play badly if he becomes upset, and you'll lose just as much as he will. Make it a partnership rule to jot important hands down on a piece of paper so that you can reserve any discussion until the evening's bridge game is over.

It's also important to understand that some bridge disasters may be *errors of partnership* rather than the fault of any individual. Suppose partner opens with Two Diamonds, you pass because you think he has a "modern" weak two-bid, and he turns up with a strong-two bid! Instead of reaching your laydown game (or slam), you languish in a partial. This is admittedly an unhappy result, but there's no point in screaming angrily at each other to try and affix the blame. Your side should have clearly agreed upon your bidding methods before beginning play, and the important lesson to learn is that you both must discuss matters more carefully before the next game begins.

Finally, *don't* be a "results player." Anyone can tell what the *winning* play is after the deal is over, but that doesn't make it the *correct* choice:

DUMMY

♣ A Q J 10 2

WEST   EAST

♣ 9 8 7 3   ♣ K

DECLARER

♣ 6 5 4

When missing five cards including the King, the right play is to finesse. It's easy to see that this plan is singularly unsuccessful as the cards lie, but don't be depressed if you go wrong (and don't yell at partner if he elects to finesse!). Bridge does involve some luck, and trying for perfection on every deal will simply spoil your own fun— and everyone else's.

RECOMMENDED READING

The proper play may lose on any one deal, but will bring you out well ahead in the long run. If you consistently lose at bridge, however, you probably *are* doing some things wrong. No one ever became a good bridge player overnight (or even in several months), so there's no reason to be discouraged, but you should try to improve your game by reading as well as playing. Of the many bridge books now on the market, the best one on intermediate card play and defense is Victor Mollo and Nico Gardener's *Card Play Technique: The Art of Being Lucky* (Newnes, 1955). *Goren's Bridge Complete* (Doubleday,

1973) is a comprehensive treatment of all phases of bridge by the game's best-known expert. If you're looking for a complete coverage of bridge in dictionary form, you'll want *The Official Encyclopedia of Bridge* (Crown, 1971). Finally, my own *Bridge: A Concise Guide* (Franklin Watts, 1975) is a brief collection of tips for those who don't have time to read more lengthy tomes, and includes a comprehensive list of suggested readings for those who do.

ANY QUESTIONS?

In view of today's inflated prices, I feel that buyers of this book are entitled to some extra service. If you have any questions that you're still unable to answer, I'll try to clear them up for you if you send them to me *together with a stamped, self-addressed envelope.* Write to:

> Bob Ewen
> 8101 Camino Real
> Apt. C-317
> Miami, Fla. 33143

In the interest of self-preservation, I must reserve the right to withdraw this offer at any time without notice, and to refuse to answer any question for any reason (as for example if it will require 14 single-spaced typewritten pages!).

Good luck—and have fun!

BRIDGE MOVIE 5: "DEE-FENSE!"

East deals and opens the bidding with One Heart, and you (South) hold:

♠ A K J 2
♡ 6 2
◇ K 9 5
♣ K 7 4 3

What call do you make?

ANSWER: Double. You have a hand worth an opening bid and fine support for all unbid suits, so ask partner to pick the one that he prefers.

West raises to Two Hearts, North passes, and East jumps to Four Hearts. *What now?*

ANSWER: Pass. You have told your story and partner appears to be broke, so a graceful retreat is indicated.

West and North also pass, ending the auction. *What card do you lead?*

ANSWER: The King of Spades. This fine attacking lead is unlikely to do declarer any favors, so it has everything to gain and little to lose.

West puts down the following dummy:

NORTH (PARTNER)

WEST (DUMMY)   EAST (DECLARER)

♠ Q 8 7
♡ 9 8 7 5   ♠ K led
◇ A J 7 2   by you
♣ 10 8

SOUTH (YOU)
♠ A J 2
♡ 6 2
◇ K 9 5
♣ K 7 4 3

Dummy's Seven of Spades is played, partner contributes the Nine of Spades, and declarer follows with the Spade Four.

What do you lead to the next trick?

ANSWER: The Ace of Spades. Partner's unusually high Spade spot asks you to continue the suit, so cash your other winner.

Dummy plays the Eight of Spades on your Ace, partner follows with the Three of Spades, and declarer plays the Five of Spades. The current situation is:

NORTH (PARTNER)

WEST (DUMMY)   EAST (DECLARER)
♠ Q
♡ 9 8 7 5
◇ A J 7 2
♣ 10 8

SOUTH (YOU)
♠ J 2
♡ 6 2
◇ K 9 5
♣ K 7 4 3

Now what do you lead?

ANSWER: The Two of Spades. Partner's high-low urgently requests that you play a third round of Spades. He probably began with a doubleton Spade and wishes to ruff away dummy's Queen, and your Jack of Spades should be preserved for use later on.

Dummy tops your deuce with the Queen of Spades, partner justifies his existence (and his signals) by producing the Three of Hearts, and declarer unhappily plays the Six of Spades. You now have three tricks in the bag and need only one more to defeat the contract, and partner tries to help out by returning the Five of Clubs. Declarer hops up with the Ace, and you properly signal your enthusiasm for Clubs by playing the Seven-spot. East quickly draws trumps by cashing the Ace and King of Hearts, you and dummy play two small Hearts, and North contributes the Heart Four and Club Two.

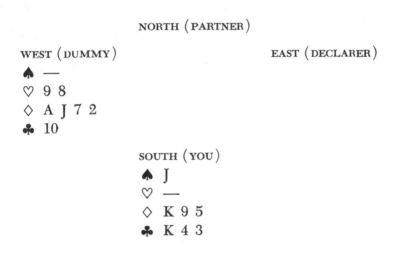

NORTH (PARTNER)

WEST (DUMMY)   EAST (DECLARER)
♠ —
♡ 9 8
◊ A J 7 2
♣ 10

SOUTH (YOU)
♠ J
♡ —
◊ K 9 5
♣ K 4 3

East now leads the Queen of Diamonds. *Do you cover with your King?*

ANSWER: Yes. If declarer has the Ten of Diamonds as well as the Queen, your King is lost regardless of what you do; but if he has Q x or Q x x in Diamonds, failing to cover will give him three Diamond tricks instead of two.

East tops your King with dummy's Ace and leads the Eight of Hearts. He overtakes this with the Heart Queen, and you discard a small Club. The remaining cards are:

NORTH (PARTNER)

WEST (DUMMY)   EAST (DECLARER)
♠ —
♡ 9
◇ J 7 2
♣ 10

SOUTH (YOU)
♠ J
♡ —
◇ 9 5
♣ K 4

East now leads the Ten of Spades and you produce your carefully preserved Jack, forcing him to ruff with dummy's Nine of Hearts. He cashes dummy's Jack of Diamonds, leads a small Diamond and ruffs it in his hand, and plays the Jack of Hearts. However, all this only delays the inevitable. His last card is the Jack of Clubs, and you capture it with your King to score the vital setting trick. (And partner proves that he is also on the ball, for his remaining card is the Queen of Clubs!) Here's the complete deal:

NORTH
♠ 9 3
♡ 4 3
◇ 10 8 6 4
♣ Q 9 6 5 2

WEST
♠ Q 8 7
♡ 9 8 7 5
◇ A J 7 2
♣ 10 8

EAST
♠ 10 6 5 4
♡ A K Q J 10
◇ Q 3
♣ A J

SOUTH
♠ A K J 2
♡ 6 2
◇ K 9 5
♣ K 7 4 3

SOUTH	WEST	NORTH	EAST
—	—	—	1 ♡
Double	2 ♡	Pass	4 ♡
Pass	Pass	Pass	

East will make his contract if you fail to give partner a Spade ruff, for you'll collect only two Spade tricks and one Club trick. (Even if you never lead Spades, East can eventually lead up to dummy's Queen twice and force you to commit yourself first.) If you part with your Jack of Spades too soon, declarer will bring home his game by leading the Ten of Spades and discarding a Club from dummy. And if you fail to cover the Queen of Diamonds, East will finesse dummy's Jack on the next round and get rid of his Jack of Clubs on dummy's Diamond Ace. Declarer does gain some consolation by scoring 150 honors, but he would have won much more had you failed to put up such a strong "dee-fense!"

Scoring Table

I. TRICKS *BID FOR AND MADE* (scored *below the line*)

Denomination | Score for *Each Trick above Book*

Notrump (NT) — 40 for first; 30 for each other
Major suit (♠ or ♡) — 30 for each
Minor suit (◇ or ♣) — 20 for each

Notes: (1) If final contract is *doubled*, multiply above values by 2; if final contract is *redoubled*, multiply above values by 4.

(2) *Game* equals 100 points *below the line*. It may be made in a single deal; or, provided that the opponents do not make game in the meantime, by building up two or more *part-scores* that total 100 points. When game is made, a new horizontal line is drawn, and each side needs 100 points *below the line* to win the next game. The first side to win *two* games wins the *rubber*.

II. OVERTRICKS (scored *above the line*)

Not Vulnerable   Vulnerable

	Not Vulnerable	Vulnerable
Undoubled	Same as trick value	
Doubled	100 each	200 each
Redoubled	200 each	400 each

III. BONUSES (scored *above the line*)

1. Rubber Bonus: 700 if opponents are not vulnerable
   500 if opponents are vulnerable

2. Slam Bonus: 500 for small slam if you are not vulnerable
   750 for small slam if you are vulnerable
   1000 for grand slam if you are not vulnerable
   1500 for grand slam if you are vulnerable

3. Honors Bonus: 100 for four trump honors *in one hand*
   150 for all five trump honors *in one hand*
   150 for four Aces at Notrump *in one hand*

4. Special Bonus: 50 for making any doubled or redoubled contract

5. Unfinished
   Rubber Bonus: 300 for a game
   50 for a part-score

IV. PENALTIES FOR FAILING TO FULFILL A CONTRACT (scored *above the line*)

Fail by	Not Vulnerable Undoubled	Doubled	Vulnerable Undoubled	Doubled
1 trick	50	100	100	200
2 tricks	100	300	200	500
3 tricks	150	500	300	800
4 tricks	200	700	400	1100
5 tricks	250	900	500	1400
Each extra undertrick	50	200	100	300

Notes: (1) If contract is *redoubled*, multiply doubled value by 2.

(2) A side is *vulnerable* if it has won one game; a side is *not vulnerable* if it has *not* won one game.

V. DETERMINING THE WINNER

When a rubber is completed, the winner is determined by adding up *all* points scored by each side (*including* "wiped-out" partials) and subtracting the smaller total from the larger one. It is possible for the partnership winning the rubber bonus to wind up as the losers (for example, they may have incurred a number of costly penalties). Several rubbers are usually played during one session, and the overall winner is the partnership (or person, if partnerships have been changed) scoring the most points.

Glossary

Above the line. The place where points that *don't* count towards game are scored. Overtricks, bonuses, and penalties are scored above the line.

Active defense. Taking risks in order to try and defeat a contract quickly, because it is apparent that declarer will be able to develop enough tricks if given time to do so.

Artificial bid. *See* **conventional bid.**

Auction. *See* **bidding.**

Back score. A score sheet on which each player is listed individually, so that his results during different rubbers with different partners may be tallied.

Balanced hand (or **balanced suit distribution**). A hand with 4-3-3-3, 4-4-3-2, or 5-3-3-2 suit distribution; thus, a hand with no more than one Distribution Point.

Below the line. The place where points that count towards game are scored. Only points for tricks *bid for and made* are scored below the line.

Bid. A number from one to seven combined with a denomination (one of the four suits or Notrump).

Bidding. The first stage of a deal of bridge, during which players compete for the right to name the contract.

Bidding system. An agreement between two partners about the meaning of the many different bids that they may make.

Blackwood convention. A procedure for discovering how many Aces and Kings partner holds; used to investigate chances for slam.

Board. (1) A synonym for **dummy**. (2) In duplicate bridge, the device which retains a deal intact after it has been played so that it can be used again at other tables.

Book. The first six tricks taken by declarer, which do *not* count against the number specified by his contract.

Break. How the cards in a particular suit are divided between the enemy hands.

Business double. *See* **penalty double.**

Bust. A very bad hand.

Call. A bid, pass, double, or redouble.

Card. One of the 52 items that comprise the deck.

Cash. Lead a card that cannot be defeated, thereby winning the trick.

Closed hand. A synonym for declarer's hand.

Clubs. The lowest-ranking suit, symbolized by ♣. A minor suit.

Cold. *See* **laydown.**

Contested auction. An auction in which both partnerships make at least one bid.

Contract. The bid just prior to the three passes that end the auction. The contract specifies how many tricks declarer must take and the trump suit (if any).

Contract bridge. A term used to distinguish the modern form of bridge from an earlier version (called **auction bridge**) in which all tricks counted towards game regardless of whether or not they were bid for.

Control. *See* **first-round control; second-round control; third-round control.**

Conventional bid. A bid that, by partnership agreement, does *not* necessarily show any strength or interest in the denomination named in that bid.

Cover. Play a higher card than one just played by an opponent.

Crossruff. Trump one suit in dummy and a different suit in

declarer's hand, back and forth, thereby scoring a trick
with each trump owned by declarer's side.

Cue-bid. (1) A bid in a suit bid by the opponents. (2) A
bid that shows some strength in the denomination named
in that bid, but no desire to play in that denomination.

Cut. Place about the top half of the deck on the table, and then
put what was formerly the bottom of the deck on top.

Danger hand. A defender who can jeopardize the contract if
he gains the lead, whereas his partner cannot.

Deal. (1) The basic unit in bridge, consisting of the bidding
and play. (2) Distribute the cards to each player.

Dealer. The player who distributes the cards to each player,
and who begins the auction.

Deck. The group of 52 cards, consisting of four suits (Spades,
Hearts, Diamonds, and Clubs) of 13 cards each (Ace
through deuce).

Declarer. The member of the partnership buying the contract
who *first* bid the denomination named in that contract. The
declarer plays both his hand and that of his partner (the
dummy).

Defender. An opponent of the declarer.

Denomination. Notrump, Spades, Hearts, Diamonds, or Clubs.

Diamonds. The next-to-lowest-ranking suit, symbolized by ◊.
A minor suit.

Discard. A played card that is *not* of the same suit as the one
led and *not* a trump. A discard cannot win a trick.

Distribution. (1) The number of cards in each suit held by one
player. (2) The way in which one particular suit is divided
among the four players.

Distribution Points (DP). A numerical method for estimating
the trick-taking potential of short suits at suit contracts. The
shorter the suit, the sooner the player will be able to ruff
and hence the more DP.

Double. A call that increases the scoring if the doubled bid
becomes the final contract. Only a bid by an opponent may
be doubled.

Double finesse. A finesse that is executed against *two* higher cards held by the opponents.

Double raise. A bid of a suit first named by partner that is made at a level one higher than the legal minimum.

Doubleton. A two-card suit.

Down. *See* set.

Draw trumps. Play enough rounds of trumps to exhaust the opponents' supply.

Duck. Play a smaller card than did an opponent, although holding a higher one.

Dummy. Declarer's partner, whose hand is exposed during the play.

Duplicate bridge. A form of tournament bridge in which a number of tables play the same deals.

Duplication of values. Apparent values that fail to take tricks because they clash with partner's values in the same suit.

Echo. Playing a higher spot card before a smaller one; used by a defender to encourage partner to lead that suit, or to show an even number of cards in that suit, or (if in the trump suit) to show possession of a third trump.

Enter. Make a play which gives partner the lead.

Entry. A card that will gain the lead for its holder because it is certain to win a trick.

Equals. Cards next to one another in rank (such as Q J 10), which are equal in trick-taking power when held by the same player.

Establish. Turn lower cards into winners, as by driving out all of the other cards in that suit.

Exit. A play which deliberately surrenders the lead to the other partnership.

Extra tricks. *See* overtricks.

False card. An unusual play made to deceive an opponent.

Finesse. An attempt to win a trick with a card that is smaller than one still held by the enemy.

First-round control. The ability to prevent the opponents from taking any tricks in that suit; an Ace or (at a suit contract) a void.

Fit. A hand that meshes well with partner's, such as one with length in his suggested trump suit.

Five-card majors. A partnership agreement that an opening bid of One Heart or One Spade promises at least five cards in the suit bid.

Follow suit. Play a card of the same suit as the one led; must be done if possible.

Forcing bid. A bid that asks partner not to pass at his next turn unless the opponent prior to him make a bid.

Forcing situation (or **forcing auction**). A situation during the auction in which a player should not pass, even if he does not like his hand, because partner's previous bidding requests that he be given at least one more chance to speak.

Forcing to game. A situation during the auction in which neither partner should pass until game has been bid.

Freak hand. A hand that is extremely unbalanced.

Game. A score of 100 points or more below the line.

Game contract. A contract which, if made, will produce at least 100 points below the line.

Grand slam. A contract requiring all thirteen tricks; a seven-bid.

Hand. (1) The 13 cards held by any one player. (2) The order in which a person plays to a trick; thus, "second hand" is the second person to play to that trick.

Hearts. The second-highest-ranking suit, symbolized by ♡. A major suit.

High-card points (HCP). A numerical method for estimating the trick-taking potential of high cards. The higher the card, the more likely it is to take a trick and hence the more HCP. HCP are counted only for the four highest honors.

High-low. *See* **echo.**

Hold up. Refuse to play a card that would be sure to win that trick.

Honor. Ace, King, Queen, Jack, or Ten.

Hook. *See* **finesse.**

Insufficient bid. A bid that is illegal because it does not increase the auction.

Invitational bid. A bid that asks partner to go on to game (or slam) if he has maximum values for his previous bidding.

Jump bid. A bid at least one level higher than the legal minimum.

Jump raise. A jump bid in a suit first bid by partner.

Jump shift. A jump bid in a suit that neither partner has bid before.

Kibitzer. Spectator at a bridge game.

Laydown. Said of a contract that is easy to make regardless of how the enemy cards are distributed.

Lead. The first card played to a trick, to which the other players must follow suit if they can.

Length. The number of cards a player holds in a particular suit.

Length points (LP). A numerical method for estimating the trick-taking potential of long suits. The longer (and stronger) the suit, the more likely it is that the small cards in that suit will be able to take tricks and hence the more LP.

Level of bidding. The number part of a bid.

LHO. An abbreviation for "Left-Hand Opponent."

Limited bid. A bid that precisely defines the strength and distribution of a hand.

Little slam. *See* small slam.

Loser. A card that cannot possibly take a trick, or be won by partner, when that suit is led.

Major suit. Spades or Hearts.

Maximum. A hand at the upper limit of the range of strength promised by the previous bidding.

Minimum. A hand at the lower limit of the range of strength promised by the previous bidding.

Minor suit. Diamonds or Clubs.

Misfit. A situation where each partner has great length in the other one's short suits, making it impossible to find a good trump suit even though both hands are unbalanced.

Natural bid. A bid that shows strength and length in the denomination named in that bid; the opposite of **conventional bid.**

Negative response. A conventional response to an opening strong two-bid, showing a very weak hand.

Nonforcing bid. A bid that partner is free to pass if he doesn't like his hand.

Nonforcing situation (or **nonforcing auction**). A situation during the auction in which a player may feel free to pass, even though this risks allowing the auction to come to an end before his partner gets another chance to bid.

Notrump. The highest-ranking denomination. A Notrump contract is played without any trump suit.

Not vulnerable. Not having scored one game.

Odd tricks. Tricks taken by declarer in excess of book (six).

One hundred fifty honors. A bonus of 150 points awarded either for holding all five trump honors in one hand, or for holding all four Aces in one hand at a Notrump contract.

One hundred honors. A bonus of 100 points awarded for holding four trump honors in one hand.

Onside. Said of an enemy honor that is favorably located, as when a finesse is successful.

Opener. The player who makes the opening bid.

Opening bid. The first call other than a pass.

Opening lead. The lead to the first trick, made by the player to declarer's left before dummy is exposed.

Overbid. Bid for more tricks than is justified by the strength of one's hand.

Overcall. The first bid made by the partnership that did *not* open the bidding.

Overruff. Ruff with a higher trump after an opponent has ruffed.

Overtricks. Tricks won by declarer that are in excess of the number required for his contract.

Overtrump. *See* **overruff.**

Partnership. Two players who sit facing each other at the bridge table.

Part-score contract (or **partial**). A contract that, if made, will produce fewer than 100 points below the line.

Pass. A call indicating that a player does not bid, double, or redouble.

Passed hand. A player who had an opportunity to open the bidding, but declined to do so.

Passed out. A deal that is thrown in, without any play, because the auction begins with four consecutive passes.

Passive defense. Very cautious defense based on the belief that declarer will go down so long as the defenders don't give him any tricks to which he isn't entitled.

Penalty. Points awarded for defeating a contract.

Penalty double. A double made in the hope that the bid doubled will become the contract and a sizable set will result.

Play. (1) The second stage of a deal of bridge, during which the players compete for the 13 tricks. (2) Place a card face up in the middle of the table.

Point count. A numerical estimate of the overall trick-taking potential of a hand; a summation of **high-card points, distribution points,** and **length points.**

Positive response. A response to an opening strong two-bid that shows some values; the opposite of **negative response.**

Power winners. Cards that can take tricks without any prior preparation, such as an Ace or the A K or A K Q in the same suit.

Preemptive bid. A bid made at an extremely high level in order to disrupt the enemy auction, showing a long and strong suit and little defensive strength.

Promotion. Turning a card into a winner by driving out the higher card in that suit.

Proprieties. Rules of bridge that refer to the way in which calls and plays should be made.

Psychic bid. A bid that deliberately gives wrong information about a hand in order to fool the opponents.

Raise. Bid a suit that was first bid by partner.

Rank. (1) The priority of each suit during the auction and during the cut for partners. (2) The trick-taking power of the cards within each suit.

Rebid. A player's second bid.

Redouble. A call, made after an enemy double, that will further increase the scoring if the redoubled bid becomes the contract.

Responder. The partner of the player who opens the bidding.

Review the bidding. A request to have all previous calls repeated in order; legal whenever it is a player's turn to bid.

Revoke. Fail to follow suit when able to do so; an illegal play.

RHO. An abbreviation for "Right-Hand Opponent."

Rockcrusher. A very powerful hand.

Rubber. A single contest of bridge, won by the first partnership to make two **games**.

Rubber bonus. An award for winning two games before the opponents do, equal to 700 points if the opponents are not vulnerable and 500 points if they are vulnerable.

Ruff. Play a trump when a side suit is led; legal only if void of the suit led.

Ruff and discard (or **ruff and sluff**). Occurs when declarer and dummy are both void of the suit led, and one hand trumps while the other gets rid of a side-suit card (usually a loser).

Ruffing finesse. A finesse that, if successful, is won by either the card led or by trumping a higher card played by an opponent.

Sacrifice. A bid made even though the player expects to go down if it becomes the contract, because he believes that the penalty will be considerably less than what the opponents will score if they are allowed to buy the contract.

Second-round control. The ability to prevent the opponents from taking more than one trick in that suit; a King or (at a suit contract) a singleton.

Sequence. *See* **equals**.

Set. Said of a contract that is *not* made; defeated.

Show out. Fail to follow suit.

Shuffle. Mix the cards thoroughly prior to dealing.

Side. *See* **partnership.**

Side suit. During a deal played at a suit contract, any non-trump suit.

Signals. Plays made by the defenders in order to exchange information about their hands.

Signoff. A bid that orders partner to pass.

Simple bid. A bid at the minimum legal level; the opposite of **jump bid.**

Singleton. A one-card suit.

Slam. A contract requiring twelve or thirteen tricks; a six-bid or seven-bid.

Sluff. *See* **discard.**

Small slam. A contract requiring twelve tricks; a six-bid.

Spades. The highest-ranking suit, symbolized by ♠. A major suit.

Split. (1) A synonym for **break.** (2) Play one of two or more equal honors.

Spot card. Nine, Eight, Seven, Six, Five, Four, Three, or Two.

Stayman convention. A conventional procedure for discovering whether or not a player who opens the bidding with One (or more) Notrump holds a four-card major suit.

Stopper. A holding that figures to prevent the opponents from enjoying an uninterrupted run of winners in that suit; the Ace or a *protected* lower honor (K x, Q x x, J x x x, or better).

Strong two-bid. An opening bid of two of a suit that shows an extremely powerful hand and orders partner not to pass.

Suit. Spades, Hearts, Diamonds, or Clubs.

Support. (1) Holding in a suit first bid by partner. (2) Bid a suit first bid by partner.

Takeout double. A double that asks partner to bid his best unbid suit, and is therefore *not* an attempt to penalize the enemy.

Tenace. Two or more honors in one hand (or one partnership) that are not equals.

Third-round control. The ability to prevent the opponents from taking more than two tricks in that suit; a Queen or (at a suit contract) a doubleton.

Trick. A group of four cards, one played by each participant.

Tripleton. A three-card suit.

Trump. A card in one particular suit, designated during the bidding, that outranks any card of a different suit.

Trump a trick. *See* ruff.

Trump suit. The suit named in any contract that is not a Notrump contract.

Two-way finesse. A position in which declarer can finesse either opponent for the missing high card.

Unbalanced hand (or **unbalanced suit distribution**). A hand with at least two Distribution Points; any hand with at least two doubletons, or at least one singleton, or at least one void.

Unbid suit. A suit not (yet) bid during the auction.

Unblocking. Playing higher cards than necessary so that the lead won't end up in the wrong hand at the crucial moment.

Uncontested auction. An auction in which only one partnership bids.

Underbid. Bid for fewer tricks than is justified by the strength of one's hand.

Undertricks. Tricks that declarer needed to make his contract, but failed to win.

Unlimited bid. A bid that does *not* precisely define the strength and distribution of a hand.

Void. Having no cards in a suit.

Vulnerable. Having scored one game.

Weak two-bid. An opening bid of two of a suit that, by prior agreement between partners, is preemptive and does *not* show a strong hand.

Winner. A card that will take a trick.

Working honor. An honor held by declarer's side that is of value during the play; one that does *not* fall victim to duplication of values.